FROM ONE MOTHER TO ANOTHER

LIVING WITH POSTPARTUM DEPRESSION

Chelsea Jaskolski

Author's Note

The information provided in this book, the story, and its interpretation come from my own personal experience living with postpartum depression, my personal medical records, and further research. The thoughts, views and opinions are solely mine and are not necessarily reflective of my employer or any groups or individuals affiliated with me. This book is not intended as definitive truth; it is opinion based on my knowledge and understanding. I am not officially diagnosing any individual with a mental illness. I drafted this book with the goal of understanding further cases of postpartum depression and hope other woman will seek help for themselves or someone they know who may be struggling.

Table of Contents

INTRODUCTION

As I sat on the sage-green sofa next to my best friend, I looked out the balcony of her two-bedroom condo, my gaze focused somewhere amidst the snow-covered trees of a sleepy town near to where I grew up. The mild sun cast a warm gaze on the tan walls surrounding us and the chatter of daytime television hung in the background and a calm flicker of the fireplace blazed in the corner of her open-concept floor plan. She held her new baby girl in her arms, sharing story after story of all events leading to this moment in time: when she first realized she was in labor, her trip to the hospital, the epidural and delivery, and of course, the midnight feedings she had endured since returning home from the hospital. Throughout the conversation, she occasionally looked from me to the baby and produced a smile that lit up the room. The pride she had for creating this tiny human and pure joy she felt was obvious.

Although I knew we were conversing, I'm being honest when I say that I cannot remember one comprehensible word of the hour-long conversation. Having been friends for over two decades, it saddens me to admit that. We have known each other since the fourth grade, were each other's maid of honor, and to this day routinely try to catch up whenever or wherever we get the opportunity. One would assume I should have been able to talk to her about anything. But I didn't, not this.

I watched her, with obvious intent, as she held her baby with a love that radiated from within. Of my handful of close friends, Adrianne was one of the first to birth a child. I'd given birth almost 15 months prior to this conversation, but I had a lingering feeling that there might be something amiss with myself, as the way I felt after I had my son, Nathan, resembled nothing like what I was seeing based on Adrienne's actions. Sure, it could all be an act, but that was highly unlikely: she wasn't an actor, and she certainly wasn't one to put on a show for my entertainment.

How I felt after Nathan was born was different from what has always been portrayed by new mothers. When I saw mothers on television or in the movies give birth, they always shed tears of joy the minute the baby was out. They expressed this longing of love for their new baby, as if they couldn't remember the days before the baby was born. In real life, new moms post on social media hours and days after giving birth, saying how they are beyond grateful for this journey, wishing their baby wouldn't grow so fast, and feeling so blessed to be this new child's mother.

I certainly didn't fall into that category. I knew I felt different, but at 24, recently divorced and a new mother, I didn't know if it was because of my inherent personality, because of my age, or for some other reason. I had heard of postpartum depression, but when I filled out the questionnaire at my six-week postpartum checkup, I passed with excellence. But to this day, if you talk to Ady, she will tell you that she'll never forget the look on my face when I finally asked the question that had been burning a hole in my brain since minutes after Nathan was born.

"How are you so happy?"

That simple thought kept me up at night. Why did other mothers seem so joyful? That question made me doubt everything about who I was and what kind of mother I wanted to be, but for some reason I couldn't find the desire within myself to bring it to fruition. When I think back to the day I met my best friend's daughter Aubree for the first time, the memory ends right there, with that question: How are you so happy? I know from recollections with her that we in fact did speak about the matter further, but I cannot recall what that entailed. I don't know what words of advice she gave me or if in fact she gave me any at all. I don't even know if I offered up anything other than that question or if we just stared at each other until I went home. It's as if I blocked that memory from even my deepest thoughts. I image on her end there must have been some shock, as what I was asking was way in left field. I was asking her why she was happy as she held her healthy, beautiful baby girl in her arms.

I had longed to have the connection with my son that she appeared to have with her weeks-old daughter, and Nathan was already over a year old. I was dying to know what the secret was, what I could do to get what she had, and I was desperately hoping she would give me the answer that I was looking for. I wanted a magic pill that would make everything better. The love and absolute joy she felt when looking into her precious baby's eyes was palpable and I was envious to experience the same. This isn't to say that I didn't love my son, because I absolutely know that somewhere deep inside me, I did; I just didn't know what that felt like, and my behavior didn't align with other new mothers' when compared side by side. I didn't have a desire to spend my days and evenings side by side with my new baby. I couldn't find joy and be present in the moment and was always looking to "what's next." I hoped that maybe I would feel different when the next milestone came. I know that I didn't want anything bad to happen to Nathan. He was a part of me, but sadly, I needed clarification on how I should feel and if it was OK to feel that way.

What is considered normal behavior for a new mother? Is there a normal? Were my actions and feelings of emptiness and sometimes sadness confirmed? Did all mothers feel this way? Did I need counseling or medication? How am I supposed to feel? Is there something wrong with me? What happens if something is wrong with me? Should I tell someone? Will they judge me? Do all new moms feel an instant connection to their baby? If they don't, then when do they?

The only thing I knew about having a baby was that it was lonely. I was tired of fighting and hiding and pretending that everything was OK when it wasn't. I didn't know how to fix it, but I was too scared to talk to anyone. Ady was the first person that I felt I could really even ask this very raw question, and even then, I had waited a long 15 months until her daughter was born before I had even contemplated bringing it up. I was a twice-married 24-year-old with a toddler and two step-kids. I was the oldest of three children. Mothering should have been a natural transition, but for some reason it wasn't.

Sadly, I would struggle for almost another full year before things improved, only to experience another bout of postpartum depression after the birth of my third child, Nadia. It took several years after Nathan was born to realize that what I was dealing was something that also affects many other women across the world. Although it didn't take me nearly as long to put two and two together after Nadia was born, postpartum depression still affected me and my loved ones lives' dramatically. Even though postpartum depression doesn't look the same for everyone and I certainly wasn't the first nor the last to receive this diagnosis, it certainly felt that way.

CHAPTER ONE

I'm a Mom Now

It wasn't one defining moment but rather a conglomeration of events that led me to the thought, "Is this it? Is this what being a mother feels like?" It couldn't be, because if it was, every movie I had watched and every country song I had ever listened to had been lying to me for as long as I could remember.

So many songs and so many movies all seem to follow a similar path. The characters meet early on in the movie but end up going their separate ways, only to reconnect years later, get married, and start a family. I mean, the movies *When Harry Met Sally*, *Notting Hill*, or heck, even *Life as We Know It* speak for themselves. If those aren't perfect rom-coms, I don't know what is. The movie usually ends with the husband admiring his partner from afar while she holds a new baby or a pregnant belly, and a proud smile spreads across his face. As the camera pans out or the last set of lyrics sets in, we get another glimpse of their house in the suburbs, surrounded by a white picket fence and a walkway lined with beautiful rose bushes. I'm feeling *Father of the Bride* vibes here. A perfectly content ending to a fairytale story.

By the time I had Nathan at age 24, I had already married and separated from my high school sweetheart, and to say I met Nathan's father, my husband, under any romantic conditions would be a straight up lie. It was love at first sight, that's for sure—there's no denying that, for either one of us—but it definitely started out messy. We didn't meet years before we got together. We didn't have a house with a white picket fence, much less a down payment for one. We were lucky if we could make rent on time.

When I met Dave, he already had two children. I knew that I wanted to have a child, and I also knew that my ob-gyn wasn't even sure having more than one child was a possibility. She also was very candid that time wasn't on my side. When I saw how Dave treated his kids, I fell for him even harder than I already had. I knew full on that if our relationship didn't work, I could trust this man with my child when I wasn't around, and I had never had that feeling before.

At my core, I am a planner; I am organized, and I am put-together. I know what I'm doing and why I'm doing it. I have a purpose. My house is decorated perfectly to my style and at any given moment, without any notice, a Realtor could walk in and show said house to a potential buyer. Does this make me a perfectionist with unattainable goals? Maybe, but I know that when I make a decision, it will be executed to the best of my abilities. For me, that's what makes my story so gut-wrenching. I was not at my best for the first two years Nathan was alive, and not only was I not at my best for this sweet little boy who loved his mother, but that I knew something was wrong and I didn't get help. I also have a tendency, especially as I get older, to know in my gut if the decision I am making is or isn't a good one, with the hardest part simply deciding if I follow my gut or not. What if my gut is wrong? (Spoiler alert, always follow your gut—and that isn't a suggestion.) When and if I decide to do something, I do it with serious conviction. I don't do anything halfway.

When I decided to get pregnant, I began to put a plan in place. I knew what Nathan's name was going to be and how the next several years of my life and his were going to play out. Unfortunately—or fortunately, depending on how you look at things—I was about to learn an exceedingly difficult lesson: life doesn't always go as planned. Mind you, it's a lesson that's so obvious I thought I didn't need to learn it, but I was wrong. You can manifest something all you want, and I do believe there is power in manifestation, but even if you put that shit into the universe until you're blue in the face, it doesn't necessarily mean things will turn out exactly as you hoped. For me, having a child was so far from the image I envisioned it to be, so different from what I dreamed it was, and not even remotely close to what I had believed to be true.

When Nathan was born, close to our one-year dating anniversary, I was given a rude wakeup call. My reality was not panning out like what I saw in the movies. I know that sounds naive, even as I type it, but I really had no idea what I was in for. Talking about the changes your mind and body goes through after you have a child and what life was like having a baby at home was not something that happened organically with my mother and me. Sure, she would tell me funny stories here and there about how fussy I was or how sleep deprived she was, but they all seemingly ended the same; she was honored to be my mother and none of the troubles ever amounted to anything serious. Comparatively, Nathan was an easy baby, everyone thought so. He slept through the night most days of the week and kept himself occupied and entertained by even the smallest of things. So many of my friends and family told me how lucky I was to have such a good baby, but I, unfortunately, still found myself distant from him.

I had all the things that you could need to care for a baby. My mother threw me a baby shower about a month before Nathan was born. I received so many wonderful gifts from my family and friends as well as many gifts from my mother's longtime friends. My aunt gave me a crib, my grandmother purchased Nathan's dresser, and a group of coworkers got together and purchased the changing table. I had enough bottles to fill a cabinet, and so many boxes of diapers and wipes, I wasn't sure I would be able to use them all. I received so many clothes that Nathan didn't even get the chance to wear some of them. Of course, having all these things made caring for Nathan easier physically, but it didn't make things easier mentally.

What I thought motherhood was going to be like and what motherhood was actually like for me were two vastly different scenarios, and I couldn't relate to either one of them. I had painted a picture of how having a baby should look, and when the colors didn't blend seamlessly, I didn't know how to cope with it. The state of my mental health after giving birth was unrecognizable, and what I was experiencing postpartum was not even close to what I was psychologically ready for. Every day, I would tell myself something new, tell myself a little lie, to justify my feelings and actions to myself—and, I suppose, to others.

While I heard of postpartum depression at my six-week checkup, it wasn't a conversation that was heavily focused on since my screening questionnaire didn't raise any red flags. Additionally, I didn't really know what symptoms would be classified as postpartum depression, so leading up to that physicians appointment, I hadn't really been prepared to talk about how I had been feeling mentally. I assumed the check-up was to focus more heavily on my physical well-being, in which I was prepared to talk about.

I certainly didn't know anyone who experienced postpartum depression, much less talk about it. Naturally, I am someone who likes to have control of my life, my decisions, and suddenly I had neither. I wasn't in control of my body anymore. I wasn't in control of my feelings or my hormones, and I certainly wasn't in control of what my days would consist of.

I was always tired and as someone who loved working 2nd shift, because it allowed me to maximize the number of hours I slept each night, I found that working from 2:00 p.m. to 10:00 p.m. to be exhausting now that I had a baby. I couldn't sleep all morning, go to work, then come home and binge watch *Nip/Tuck* on Netflix. I couldn't spend hours reorganizing the kitchen cabinets or searching Pinterest for innovative ideas (my own form of self-care) in my downtime. I had a baby. A baby that now depended on me just to meet his basic needs. I was confused as to how my life suddenly was nothing like how I thought it was going to be nor anything like what it had been. I knew that having a baby was likely going to require midnight feedings, and diaper changes, but since I was never in bed by midnight as a 2nd shifter, it wasn't like this was going to interrupt my sleep. A midnight feeding really wasn't going to be a huge concern since it wasn't like I was tired at that time either. I think I downplayed in my mind how hard having a newborn baby is. I don't think I fully grasped that taking care of child was so much more than just that midnight feedings. I don't know who I thought was going to hold and feed the baby at 6 is the morning, a time when I actually was very tired. Since my normal bedtime was somewhere around 2:30 a.m., 6:00 a.m. was basically my "middle of the night."

Four or five days after Nathan was born, I sat on the edge of the bed and cried for absolutely no reason. I was sad, but I didn't understand why. It was the middle of the day, and nothing was happening. It was even sunny outside for a late October day; I remember thinking, "I can't even blame the weather." I pulled out my trusty *What to Expect When You're Expecting* book and realized I was experiencing what is often referred to as the "baby blues" and that feeling sadness was in fact a very normal reaction after having a baby. That gave me a small glimmer of hope that maybe this was just something glossed over in the movies and something new moms rarely mentioned as it is rather short lived and often inconsequential in the grand scheme of things. The baby blues were one of the last times I would recognize that my emotions were being dictated by my hormones, a chemical imbalance, or anything other than my own will. It would be one of the last times I would remember feeling much of anything, other than occasional anger, until after Nathan turned two years old.

The book recommended that you contact your health care professional if you experience sadness for longer than two weeks following the delivery of your baby, but what happens if sadness isn't what you are feeling? What happens if you don't feel like yourself, but you can't exactly pinpoint how you feel? What happens if you feel like you are watching your life as an outsider instead of an active participant? I knew things were happening as they happened, but I didn't really have any feelings about what was going on. If you don't feel any emotions, or attachment, how do you know if something is wrong? I had all these questions and more, but since I wasn't really experiencing any depression, I thought there was no real reason to visit the doctor or mention any of this to anyone. I didn't want to be the one that was different.

Postpartum depression in its simplest form, is depression that occurs after childbirth. In its most complex form, it is a mood disorder that occurs within a few weeks of giving birth, causes extreme sadness and despair, lasts longer than two weeks, and can be accompanied by a plethora of other symptoms ranging from social withdrawal, difficulty bonding with the baby, feelings of worthlessness or guilt, anxiety and/or indifference. It is a complex mix of behavioral, physical, and mental/emotional changes one might experience after giving birth. When I first came home from the hospital, I felt fine emotionally, and I was physically comfortable enough even though I had just squeezed something the size of a melon out of an opening the size of a lemon. When something didn't feel right, I would always go back to that point: I was fine when I came home from the hospital. I didn't feel overly worried about how to take care of Nathan, fretting about whether or not he was safe after laying him down for naps or bedtime. I was never concerned that I wasn't feeding him enough or that he was too hot or too cold, or that his little legs would get stuck in the side of the crib when he was sleeping. Honestly, I thought I was managing the entire situation well—except for during the baby blues.

There was one evening during those few days when Dave was working that I had called a friend, Krystal, whom I had not talked to in several months. I asked her if she could come over and stay with me while Dave was at work. He had been working second shift, which meant that I was left alone with Nathan from 1:30 p.m. until Dave got home at 10:37. I knew what route Dave took home from work and how long it would take him to get back. When I say I counted the minutes he was gone, I actually mean I was counting the minutes. Thankfully, my friend told me that she could come over before she went into work. I was so relieved, because I knew that I would be all right for at least that night. I would worry about tomorrow when tomorrow came, in hopes that these baby blues would be over by then.

I don't know why I was so anxious being home alone with Nathan, but I was, and the sheer thought of it made me want to cry even more. It didn't make sense to me. I hadn't heard of any other mothers who didn't want to be left alone with their child. When Krystal said she had to leave by 8:00 p.m. to get to the hospital on time for the start of her shift, the tears immediately started to swell in my eyes. Sure, I had a little more than two and a half hours until Dave would get home, but those two and a half hours were more than I could bear. It was a weeknight at 8:00 p.m. in the suburbs. There wasn't a whole lot going on anywhere. If I wanted to be around people, my best bet was the 24-hour Walmart about 30 minutes away, but even then, I wasn't sure I had the energy to leave the house. When she made the phone call to her employer saying that she wouldn't be in until 10:30 that night, I was thankful. To this day, it is one of the kindest things anyone has ever done for me.

Once the baby blues had ended, I was eager for any emotion that was headed my way next, because anything had to be better than being sad and crying for no reason at all. I waited and waited for the next series of emotions, but nothing ever came. Secretly, I was hoping for this strong bond that I was supposed to have with my baby, this eternal love all these new mothers talk about, but it never came. I wasn't going to tell anyone that, however. Although this deep love hadn't formed quite yet, the upside was that I didn't feel sad anymore—but I also didn't really feel happy, either. I wasn't upset and I wasn't anxious. I was just kind of just there, existing. I felt as though I were living in a life that I didn't feel one way or the other about. I was now a mother, but I didn't feel like a mother. I had this little baby that depended on me for everything, but I didn't feel honored or privileged for this new role I was given. I wasn't excited. I wasn't overjoyed.

I didn't feel this undying admiration for my child. Sure, he was adorable, and from what I am told he was the perfect baby, and yes, I loved him, but I wasn't sure if I loved him because I knew I was supposed to or because I actually did. It definitely wasn't the love that I feel for him right now as I type this. I would take a thousand bullets or a slow and painful death for any one of my children without even thinking twice if it meant they would be spared.

I would give anything to go back to that time when Nathan was a baby and do it all over again. I would love to remember more about those years without having to look at pictures to prompt my memory. The problem I had at that time was that when it came to being a mother, I could take it or leave it. I had no strong convictions about being a mother—or really about anything, for that matter. If something good happened, I would act happy, because I knew what that looked like, even though I didn't necessarily feel happy. If something sad had happened, I knew how to appear upset. If something exciting happened, I would fake enthusiasm.

For the first six or seven months of Nathan's existence, I felt disoriented and bewildered by mostly everything. I felt as though I were dead inside, hovering in purgatory, this place of existence where I went through the motions of the day just to get through it. I hoped that the way I was feeling was temporary and that I would wake up better the next morning, but I never did. I didn't know what was going on with me, but I "knew" I wasn't depressed, or so I thought. People who are depressed don't want to get out of bed, and I definitely wasn't lying around all day. I was still able to hold a full-time job and attend family functions, and my child was safe and healthy. I told myself that everything was fine, because isn't this what "normal" life looked like? I had a significant other, I lived in a good neighborhood, I had a career in x-ray doing exactly what I had gone to school for. I was living the "American Dream."

What I didn't know then was that I was entering into what would be a two-year bout of postpartum depression. This loss of emotion that I was experiencing is common for those who have gone through a traumatic experience, who are developing depression, or who are on the verge of psychosis. The emptiness I felt made it extremely difficult to bond with my baby, and even though there were so many signs suggesting postpartum depression, I didn't recognize those signs for what they were as they were happening to me.

What to take away from this chapter:

Everyone's journey after childbirth will look different. You shouldn't expect someone else's journey to be similar to your own, and just like the grieving process, there is no one right or wrong way to feel. Give yourself time and grace, because having a baby is a feat in and of itself.

Postpartum depression is not a one-size-fits-all diagnosis. Even if you don't feel sad, if you have other feelings that don't seem natural, or a lack of feelings at all, talk to a medical professional. You don't want to miss the bonding experience between you and your baby and then feel guilty later on simply because you were embarrassed to tell a physician your thoughts or feelings. Trust me when I say they have heard it all and they aren't judging you. If you feel like your physician is judging you or doesn't have empathy, you need to find a new physician.

If you are unsure whether or not you should seek the help of a qualified medical professional, another resource is a mental health hotline, such as 1-800-662-HELP. They can connect you to someone in your area and they are available 24/7/365. If you don't have health insurance, google "online counseling sessions" and start there. A reliable website to look at is medicalnewstoday.com/articles/therapy-without-insurance, which will help you get some ideas as to where to start. Additionally, betterhelp.com is another great resource.

CHAPTER TWO

Am I Depressed?

Often when people think about postpartum depression, their first thought is that the individual who is suffering is burdened with feelings of deep sadness, so much so that they cannot get out of bed or don't want to. They often think these individuals have difficulty performing routine tasks or taking care of their physical hygiene. I've often heard people give new mothers advice like "Have someone watch the baby for 15 or 30 minutes so you can take a shower and spend a few minutes doing something for yourself," or "If you're feeling down, go outside and take the baby for a walk to get some sunlight and vitamin D." Don't get me wrong, going outside and feeling the sunshine while taking a stroll with your baby is a great idea; however, it isn't necessarily going to stop you from getting postpartum depression if you're already heading down that path.

Sometimes people get postpartum depression confused with postpartum anxiety, although the two are different in that the mother or parent who has postpartum anxiety is overly anxious about things going wrong when caring for their child. They can't seem to move beyond that phase in their mind. Their worry cannot be eased, and they have difficulty sleeping because of their racing thoughts. Those with postpartum anxiety usually have a constant fear or dread that does not go away, and they can't help but think that something bad is going to happen at any given second. They often feel as though they cannot leave their baby even for the shortest amount of time because they need to have eyes on the child 24/7. These parents repeatedly find it difficult to do anything other than have a constant fixation on their child.

When comparing both of these terms, it was clear that I did not experience postpartum anxiety, but I didn't think I was experiencing postpartum depression either. A couple of times, Dave insinuated that there must be something wrong with me, as I was never really interested in performing the duties that are often associated with being a mother. I didn't have any strong feelings one way or the other about anything when it came to Nathan, except for his bedtime—and I was only fixated on that because it meant I had time to just be. If there was an opportunity to have someone else take care of my son's needs as opposed to me, I was more than happy to let them. Every once in a while, Dave would make a negative comment regarding my behavior that would make me think twice about whatever was happening in that moment, but after a few minutes of research on the internet and an online quiz to see if something was in fact "wrong" with me, I always determined that I was fine. That being said, the most frequent questions asked were usually things like: Do you feel sad more often than you did before you had your baby? *Who remembers how often they are sad? I'm not 13, I don't have a journal to reference.* Do you want to harm yourself or your baby? *Why would I want to disfigure myself in any way? Why would I want to hurt an innocent, defenseless child? What kind of question is that?* Do you have a challenging time getting out of bed in the morning? *Give me an example of someone who likes the sound of their alarm.* Do you find it difficult to enjoy activities? *I enjoy all activities that involve me either getting out of the house and not taking care of a small child, regardless of what it is.* Is it difficult to get motivated? *I am able to go to the grocery store and run errands and get to work on time. Motivation isn't an issue, especially if the task results in completion.* Do you struggle getting everyday chores or tasks done? *Nope. I get out of bed each day, shower, do the laundry and clean the dishes just as often as I did before I had Nathan.* Do you enjoy the same activities now that you did before you had your baby? *I find it difficult to enjoy a lot of things, but that's probably because I am tired. If I was able to sleep more, go to work and find some time for myself, I would definitely be going out more.*

When I answered all these questions, I always passed depression screenings fine, even though that couldn't have been further from the truth. Simply answering screening questions is just that—it's a screening. It is not meant to be used as a diagnosis, especially if that screening is answering a few questions via a quick Google search on your iPhone while your baby is napping. This isn't to say that Google is a bad place to start, but it definitely shouldn't be your main source of information or the be-all and end-all. The internet can be misleading, and deceptive, especially if you tend to find a lot of your facts on social media. This is a crucial point to remember when you are debating whether or not you have a reason to be concerned.

My son, Nathan, was born in October, right around Halloween. Even though he was born almost a month early, he was strong and healthy, and for that I am extremely grateful. I was so excited when I went into labor because that meant that my swollen feet would soon be a thing of the past, but it also meant I would soon have this little baby to love and hold. I would get to meet the love of my life and I could not wait. When I went into labor, I still had that fairytale vision of what motherhood was going to look like and I couldn't wait to get started. Forget about sleepless nights and changing diapers, I was soon going to put him in his first Halloween costume and post that shit to Facebook!

Unfortunately for me, that never came to fruition. By the time Nathan was almost one week old, he was already spending his first overnight at my parents' house. I don't remember exactly what I said to my mother that made her agree to watch her six-day-old grandchild overnight, but as I write this, I can't imagine any reason being remotely acceptable given my situation at the time. There was no trauma that occurred in which I needed daycare. I lived in a lovely home, Nathan had his own bedroom, I had reliable transportation, and I was not back to work yet. I knew that I was able to take care of my child financially and that he would live a happy life. He was surrounded by people who loved him. So why exactly was he spending the night with my parents?

It's probably clear to many of you reading this that this wasn't "normal" or rational behavior for a new mother, but for whatever reason, I couldn't see that. Most mothers fall head over heels in love with their precious child the moment that little baby is laid on their chest, and if it doesn't happen right away, it usually happens within a few hours of the baby being born. After the mother looks into their newborn baby's eyes long enough, something takes over; a love like nothing they have never felt before. They would give their life to save their child's and they would make that same decision over and over and over again if they had to. Some mothers don't even take their child out of the house for weeks or months after they are born, unless perhaps they are going to a doctor's visit. They cherish that sacred time with their new baby. The thought of giving their child to someone else to watch overnight, let alone even for a few hours shortly after being born, would be too much to bear. Having my child spend the night over at his grandparents' house one week after he was born is not typical behavior of a new mother, but not only did I not care what people thought about it, I also didn't have strong feelings about it one way or another. That strong pull between a mother and her child hadn't formed yet between Nathan and me. In my eyes, there wasn't a reason he *shouldn't* go to his grandparents' house.

Looking back, I often wonder what it was that I was thinking during that time. I know my general feelings and I have heard stories from those around me, but I really wish I would have documented my daily thoughts. I kept a pregnancy journal and a milestone journal for Nathan, but nothing documenting the average day to day tendencies. Why wasn't I worried about handing my child off to my parents for the night? Why didn't I feel a strong attachment to Nathan, and why didn't I want him to be with me?

I wish I had said something to someone about how I was feeling much earlier than I had. I believe if I would have gone into more specifics about my attitude, my actions, my behaviors, and the events that took place afterward, my story would have been much different. Even though I saw my doctor at my six-week checkup and filled out the depression screening, it didn't make much of a difference, because my behavior and the lack of feelings I showed didn't even register as a concern. Although motherhood looked much different from how I had envisioned it and how other new mothers described it to be, it didn't necessarily occur to me that those two things could be a sign that something was going on.

Whether I was unwilling to see it or unwilling to accept it is still up for debate, but I do know dismissing the emptiness inside me was my first mistake. If you ask your parents to watch the baby overnight because you need a good night's sleep, then I'm all for it. Without sleep several nights in a row, even the toughest parents will start to see cracks in the foundation. If you have the baby sleep over at your sister's so that you can spend some time with your other children and perhaps clean the house, then I say go for it. Do what is right for you and your family but understand why you are making the choices you are making or what is driving your actions. I could never justify my reasoning.

One of the things that helped me most during my time with postpartum depression was seeing a therapist. Let me emphasize something, though: I should have said seeing a *good* therapist helped me. The first therapist I saw was a train wreck. We did not agree completely, and I should have left her office after the first session, because she didn't do anything but make me feel worse about who I was as a mother and a human. Everyone's reason for seeing a therapist is different, and the goals they set for themselves while seeing a therapist are also different. That being said, you should never leave a therapist's office feeling worse about yourself. Hopeful, yes; worse, no. If anything, you should be proud of yourself for taking the first step toward healing.

Even in the year 2022, it is hard for me to admit that I saw a therapist, because I still am breaking down the barriers and stigma ingrained in me that moms have to be perfect the minute that they become a mom. Initially, I had a challenging time talking to the second therapist I saw (the good one) because I felt like I had to justify my feelings instead of working through my feelings. I didn't overly love trying to explain why I felt a certain way, because that made the entire process feel like I was playing defense instead of offense. I didn't want the therapist to think I was a bad mom for feeling what I was feeling. What I found out, though, after finally opening up, was that answering questions and talking through my feelings and my actions that followed, helped me better understand why I was feeling the way I was feeling and how those feelings and emotions dictated the manner in which I made decisions and behaved. Once I was able to understand what was driving that behavior, it was easier to correct it. Therapy also helped with coping skills in the moment because when I didn't let my emotions control the situation, I was able to get off the rollercoaster ride and think logically.

What I found out in the end is that there is no shame in living your life the way you want to live it, even if it looks different from those you love or those around you. However, if you are having a difficult time understanding why you are making the decisions you are making and can't seem to change your behavior even though you want to, then you need to address the issue by seeking the help of a professional. I couldn't tell you why I had Nathan sleep over at my parents' even though Dave and those around me thought the idea was absolutely insane. I don't necessarily think that you should base your experiences on those around you, because motherhood is not a competition, but if you think your feelings and behaviors are not in line with what your own ideals and values are normally, then it might be a promising idea to talk to someone about it. If you don't know where to start, mention it to your physician at your postpartum appointment or make an additional appointment.

What to take away from this chapter:

Don't let your emotions—or your lack of emotions—control your actions. I know this is so much easier to say than to actually do, and I still to this day struggle with this concept, but that doesn't mean we shouldn't try. Think logically about the decision you are making and don't decide in the spur of the moment simply because you are feeling one way or another or don't have an opinion about the matter. It is important to understand the why behind your decision. If you can't do that, then stop and reassess.

Seeking the help of a therapist or certified counselor does not make you any less of a mom or any less of a human than the person next to you. If you have a history of feeling better after talking through your thoughts, or if you want a deeper understanding of your emotions, a therapist or certified counselor will help you build that connection. If you don't like the therapist you are seeing, don't stick around too long. Finding someone you feel comfortable being honest with will help you get the most out of your sessions.

CHAPTER THREE

How It Started

I found out I was pregnant with Nathan on an early Sunday morning in the middle of winter. I checked myself into the local emergency department close to where Dave and I had been living at the time. We had been up since we both got off of work that evening, per usual, but this night was different, because around 3:30 in the morning, I started to experience some sharp, stabbing pains on the left side of my abdomen. I had no idea what it was, or what it could stem from, and it came out of nowhere. I had been doubled down in the fetal position lying in bed for almost 30 minutes before Dave said I should probably go to the ER. Thankfully, it wasn't exactly busy, although I can tell you from personal experience that half past three in the morning can turn into the witching hour in an emergency room, and by 4:00 a.m., all hell can break loose. Fortunately, I was able to get right back to a room and be examined. Long story short, after some labs and an ultrasound, the physician came in to discuss my results. He revealed that I was pregnant and that I had some cysts on my ovaries that were the culprit of the pain. After receiving the results, I called Dave and told him I was on my way home.

The next few days were honestly surreal. Part of me couldn't believe I was actually pregnant. *Is this really happening?* was a constant question on my mind. The real dilemma I faced, though, was telling my parents. You know when you were a kid and you had something you needed to tell your parents, but you were so nervous that you rehearsed the conversation in your mind about a hundred times before you actually got the courage to talk to them? I was 23 and still feeling that way about this conversation. Keep in mind, I had only been separated from my ex-husband for about six months when I decided to break the news to them that I was pregnant, and they had only met Dave once. I know it seemed sudden to probably everyone else, but I saw the kind of dad that he was to his other two children, and I knew he would be the same to our child. Plus, I was head over heels in love with him, and if I wanted to have kids, I had to have them sooner rather than later—and there was no better time than the present.

One Sunday evening, in spring, I went over to my parents' house for an Italian dinner. I had never before been so scared to walk into the front door of my childhood home. It was just the three of us. To this day, I can still picture myself walking into the house with the smell of garlic and oregano filling the air. I was about eight weeks pregnant at that point and I was as sick as ever. On top of having morning sickness, I was also exhausted, not only from pulling double shifts, but also from the extreme fatigue that comes your way the first trimester. I had been working for my sister at a clothing store in the mornings before I would go off to the hospital for a full eight-hour shift in the afternoons. Hilary knew I was pregnant and that I hadn't told our parents yet. She would have given anything to be a fly on the wall during that conversation.

The entire meal, I pushed my spaghetti from one side of the plate to another, taking micro bites. If you hadn't known me, you would have thought I was anorexic. The stress of separating from my prior relationship and the fact that the smell of food made me want to vomit made for one small pregnant woman. When I finally spilled the news, the only thing I remember my dad saying was, "Well, that explains why you aren't eating much." I don't know what my mother said, or if she said anything at all, but I know the evening pretty much ended there. They certainly weren't expecting that. Years later, my parents told me that after I left for the evening, they cleaned up dinner, my mom went to bed, and my dad went to the living room to watch some television. I had left them speechless.

I don't have many memories of my pregnancy back then. There are only a few that really stick out. I remember, craving Burger King cheeseburgers, and later in the pregnancy having really swollen feet. Thank God for Crocs, because I am not entirely sure how I would have found shoes wide enough for the cankles I had going on. Aside from those select few things, my memory really starts when I went into labor, which was nothing to write home about.

For about two months before I was due, Dave would remind me almost every other day that I could not go into labor on a weekend when he was scheduled to work—as if I had any control over that, you know? Apparently, his supervisor and manager at the time had some pretty strict sick call-in protocols, and if he called in on a weekend, not only would it count as a double occurrence (basically a spanking), but he was also likely going to be written up for that. Well, as sure as the sun sets in the west, I went into labor at 9:40 a.m. on a Sunday when he was scheduled to be at work at 2:00 p.m. He was pissed. And we are not just talking a little upset here, we are talking red-in-the-face, smoke-coming-out-of-his-ears pissed, and when Dave is angry, you better watch out. He will tear down anything in his path. It doesn't happen often, but when it does, you don't want to be within a thousand-mile radius of him. Far be it from me to say, but he didn't make the start of my labor experience a joyous one. It wasn't a situation where we grabbed our bags and headed toward the door with smiles on our faces and tears in our eyes as we said, "We're going to have a baby!"

When I had first met Dave in the fall of 2006, I had been in my last semester of x-ray school. It was a two-year program, which meant that five days a week, 50 weeks a year, from the hours of 7:00 a.m. to 2:30 p.m., I spent my time completing the required education that I needed to graduate as a radiology technologist. Once a week, however, instead of working day shift hours, each student in our class would have to rotate through the 1:30 p.m. to 10:00 p.m. shift, working alongside a technologist who was staffed in the emergency department. This is customary practice as it gives students the opportunity to experience the different dynamics of radiology departments depending on the day, the week, and even with whom you are working.

Dave had been the second shift lead technologist of the radiology department at that time, which meant that I would work with him every now and again. The first time he introduced himself to me, something happened; the way he shook my hand, looked into my eyes, and smiled was everything I never knew I always wanted. Even though I didn't know who he was at the time, he had known exactly who I was. Together, we were the perfect storm of misery, lust, and laughter, a combination that would be a constant in our relationship for the next decade.

I'm not sure that I know anyone that would say that the first few years we were together were happy times. The honeymoon stage of the relationship lasted a month or two, and if there wouldn't have been a baby announcement the next year, we would have never stayed together. There were many times throughout my pregnancy, and even after I gave birth to Nathan, where I am positive, we downright despised each other. We both were fresh off of prior relationships that left us emotionally scarred and not equipped to manage a new relationship. Dave was left with a couch, a mattress, and some silverware; I was still paying off the wedding to my first husband and working four part-time jobs just to make ends meet. There were now three children in the mix, and we were living in a side-by-side that we could barely afford to furnish. We had poor timing, to put it mildly, but I had gotten myself into this situation and I was going to make this relationship work.

When I brought Nathan home from the hospital, I thought that maybe something wasn't right—my gut told me something wasn't right—but at the time I wasn't exactly sure what it was. It had been 72 hours since I had Nathan and I still didn't feel any different emotionally than I did before I had him. I was missing that new mother adoration. I felt emptiness: no joy, no sadness, and no real concern or worry, and that wasn't me. I have a type A personality and have been that way for as long as I can remember. The feelings of emptiness I was experiencing were something that I was not used to. Type A individuals are ambitious, organized, usually not flexible, impatient, anxious, proactive, and concerned with time management. They also tend to be high-achieving workaholics. For those of you who have raised a tiny human, these traits often don't coincide well with a newborn.

However, after I had Nathan, I felt hardly any of these emotions. To put it simply, I didn't feel like myself. It was derealization at its finest. For the first time that I could remember, I was living life from the standpoint of someone I didn't recognize. I didn't know how to cope with the new way I was feeling, and I didn't understand why I was feeling this way. In my mind, nothing changed. I hadn't yet realized that *everything* had changed. I had a baby. I was now a mother.

I didn't know how to deal with these emotions of indifference. I wasn't able to admit to myself that I felt like I was drowning in a sea of apathy.

I was in denial about the person I thought I had to be after giving birth, because it was someone I couldn't relate to—nor did I want to. I just wanted to feel like myself again. I liked who I was prior to having a child and I wasn't interested in changing, but how could I be that person when everything was different now? Knowing that, I did the only thing that I thought would fix me and make me feel like my old self.

I went back to work.

I went back to work eight days after I had Nathan. He was born on a Sunday late afternoon, and I was back at work at 2:00 p.m. the following Monday.

When I say I went back to work, I didn't just pick up a shift here and there. I went back to 50-hour work weeks. People would ask why I came back to work so fast, and I would give one reason or another, meaningless excuses, but never the truth. As long as they didn't know the real reason I was going back to work so soon, I didn't care what they thought.

The truth was I went back to work because not only did it resemble a life I could recognize and give me a sense of being my own person again, but also, Nathan was better off with someone else than with me. When he was a baby, I didn't hover over him, and I wasn't obsessed with holding and snuggling him either. I often found creative ways where I could safely place him somewhere so that I wasn't always carrying him. I didn't have the urge to be the one to comfort him when he cried, and I didn't want to rock him to sleep, because when I wasn't working, *I* wanted to sleep. Eight hours a night just wasn't enough for me. When I had off of work, I would sleep for 12, 14, and sometimes 16 hours straight. Almost daily, when Nathan was between seven and 10 months old, I would get him out of bed in the mornings after he would wake up, which was usually around 7:15 to 7:30 a.m., set him in his exersaucer, put the television on Nickelodeon, and then go back to bed to lay down for another 45 minutes. I knew 45 minutes was the absolute longest he would stay in there before getting bored and wanting to do something else. I obviously wasn't thinking clearly nor acting rationally, as I cannot fathom actually doing this today, but I know I did, and it is one of the hardest things I have ever admitted to doing.

During this time in my life, I didn't think there were any other new mothers who felt like this. I felt so isolated, and I was ashamed to be the mom who didn't go googoo gaagaa over their new baby and being around

Nathan was a reminder of that. I was ashamed to be the mom that didn't post to social media announcing the birth of her firstborn son, with a picture and a caption that said, "Both baby and I are doing well, and I am already so in love with him." I said little because I didn't know what to say. I didn't feel vehemently invested in much of anything, nor did I have this overflowing excitement of love and desire to care for and spend time with my baby. I didn't really feel it when I was in the hospital, and I definitely didn't feel it when I got home a few days later. I knew in my heart and in my mind that I didn't want anything bad to happen to Nathan, and I knew I would never intentionally hurt him, but that summed up my feelings toward this new baby and my experience thus far. I certainly didn't feel like I was so depressed that I couldn't get out of bed, aside from just being tired all the time. I lived on Mountain Dew soda. I was more than happy to oblige when Nathan's daycare provider would call me and say that Nathan fell asleep early and that if I wanted, I could pick him up the next morning after he woke up. I was willing to let anyone watch him, whenever they wanted.

Depression and anxiety are complex subject matters in and of themselves, and although they are more openly talked about today than they have ever been before, there remains a negative connotation surrounding these topics, much like many other mental health issues. It still surprises me how extraordinarily little we know about the mind and how it works. As a society, we have studied so many other organs, have cures for so many other ailments, but we still often struggle to understand mental health. We make leaps and bounds every new year when compared to the year prior, but is that enough?

When someone speaks about postpartum depression (or postnatal depression, as it is sometimes called), there are many unknowns, even in the year 2022. It's unclear why some women experience postpartum depression and others don't, although physical, emotional, genetic, and social factors are believed to be contributors. According to the National Institute of Mental Health, risk factors include prior episodes of postpartum depression, bipolar disorder, a family history of depression, psychological stress, complications of childbirth, and a lack of support.

For me personally, there is a family history of mental health issues such as those listed. There was also an abundance of psychological stress during my pregnancy with Nathan that continued well after I had him, even though it was hard to see and name. I know how important it is to understand your medical history and what role it can play in your life, and I wish that I had known the risk factors for postpartum depression back then. If I had, I believe I would have used that knowledge as an opportunity to ask questions about the likelihood that I would suffer from it.

I wish I would have realized during the months, if not weeks or even days following Nathan's birth, that there was no need to be embarrassed about speaking honestly about my feelings—or lack thereof. As a young mom who had recently finished school, I wasn't exactly as financially stable as I would have liked to be, nor was I in an emotionally stable relationship. These factors, doubled down with my past history of depression, could have been indicators that I might be at risk for postpartum depression. I wish that I would have equated being tired all the time with depression as opposed to the exhaustion of being a new parent. I wish the lack of attachment and lack of connection to my baby had registered to me as postpartum depression.

When I take that into consideration—the fact that my hormones were playing Twister, I had a history of depression, a history of depression in my family, and I was in a tumultuous relationship—it is clear postpartum depression should have been on my radar and my physician's radar. Why hadn't I been scrutinized for this a bit more thoroughly after the delivery of my baby, given my past mental health history, and why wasn't this topic talked about before the birth? If we know PPD occurs in one out of seven women, why wasn't there more of a discussion about it? Why was it something I knew nothing about?

What to take away from this chapter:

It is unclear why some women suffer from postpartum depression, although there are risk factors that suggest some women are more susceptible than others. Examples include, an earlier history of depression and anxiety, a history of moderate to severe premenstrual syndrome, a history of sexual abuse in the past, and a negative attitude toward the recent pregnancy (Ghaedrah-

mati et. al., 2017). Other factors to consider are depression during pregnancy, anxiety during pregnancy, experiencing stressful life events during pregnancy or the early puerperium, and low levels of social support (Robertson, Wallington, and Stewart, 2004). Knowing and understanding your medical history and how it could affect your future will help supply further clarification and pinpoint things you may want to be aware of and keep an eye on.

CHAPTER FOUR

Asking For Help

As I was growing up, I had always envisioned that my husband would also be the father of my children. When I look back at my formative years, I don't remember ever thinking, "I can't wait to be a mother," but more that it was just a natural course of progression. That being said, shortly after marrying my first husband, I found out from my gynecologist that I could have difficulty carrying a child to term, especially as I got older, due to some health concerns. I vividly remember her saying that I didn't necessarily need to worry yet; however, the sooner that I have children (and decide I am finished having children), the better.

At that point in my life, I hadn't even thought about having kids. I was 21 years old. I figured I would be a young mom, because when you are 19 and in a meaningful relationship, 24 or 25 years old seems like a reasonable age to have children. Plus, my mother was that age when she had me, so it looked like a good track to follow.

The same month that I got this news from my doc, I found out that I was accepted to radiology school and would start a few months later. It was a two-year program, and there was no way I would be able to have a baby until I finished school. This, combined with the minor detail that I was married to a man I wasn't sure I wanted to be married to, meant I was in a predicament.

The semester before I graduated, I was ready to move out of my apartment with my first husband and end our relationship. If I really wanted children, then we had to be over, because I wasn't having children with him. It only took a couple of months before I realized I wanted Dave to be that person.

When Dave and I first met, I knew that something was brewing between us, but I had no idea we were going to go on the rollercoaster ride we did. I would find opportunities to switch my schedule so that I could be the student on site the same day he worked. He would find opportunities to have conversations with me whenever possible. Sometimes, we would do cases together. I saw the relationship between us grow, but I wasn't entirely confident that it would lead to anything. However, by the time I graduated, I was already in love with him.

He was funny, and not just ha-ha funny, but really, really funny! He made me smile and laugh, and I hadn't been with someone who made me laugh or smile in years. It felt so good. Sure, he had two prior relationships that didn't work out well, but he got along with Tessa's mom at the time even though they weren't together and was able to co-parent well, so that's really all I needed to know. Plus, he was a great dad. We would stay up for hours after he got home from working second shift, just doing normal adult things, like laundry, eating a late snack, and hanging out. We would watch *Project Runway*, *The Tudors*, or *Californication* and have sex for hours.

One night, as we were getting ready to go to bed, I asked him if he wanted to have a baby with me. I will admit that I had more motivation than he did, absolutely. If you were to ask Dave about this, he would say that this insanely hot 23-year-old asked him if he wanted to have a baby with her at the absolute most perfect time and he would have been off his rocker to say no. So, that was that. I went off birth control and the next month I found out I was pregnant. The way I found out I was pregnant may not have been glamourous, but it was happening, and I was happy.

While I was married to my first husband, I was deeply depressed, but I put on a show that everything was OK. I know my parents heard us fight occasionally (because we lived with them), but they didn't know the ins and outs of everything that was going on. When I met Dave, the dopamine rushes I experienced in the beginning of a new relationship put my depression on the back burner. I'm not sure it completely went away, but rather took a back seat to these new feelings. I may have thought I was cured, that I was perfectly fine, but in retrospect I don't think that was the case. The depression was definitely less prevalent, but shortly after that new infatuation subsided, those feelings of joy and happiness fell to the wayside, and the same loneliness that I felt when I was still married to my first husband started to return.

It's important to admit to yourself how you feel. Once you do that, it will be much easier to tell someone else. It's also vital that you don't assume someone else knows what you are going through. When I lived with my parents, my mother had no idea how I felt. My best friend had an inkling of how I was feeling, although I never admitted anything to her. My sister hadn't the slightest idea what was going on with me. Trust me when I say your friends and family members that are nearest and dearest to your heart do not want to see you in pain. They do not want to see you sad, and if you tell them how you are feeling, they will want to help you. And you should let them.

Most people in your life don't want to see you feeling lonely, empty, and isolated. After I had Nathan and I felt as if I was not able to bond with him fully, I kept that from everyone I knew. I was so scared of what they would think of me that I wasn't honest with myself—or anyone else, for that matter. Even though I didn't think that I could talk to my parents, my significant other, my siblings or friends, there were people in my life to whom I could have talked to, I just didn't want to out of fear and shame. The wonderful thing about the internet is that you can find help almost anywhere. If you don't feel comfortable talking to a friend or loved one, there are many virtual support groups and resources that you likely don't even know about. You can also always talk to your doctor. Your physician wants the days, weeks, and months following the birth of your baby to be as pleasant and as memorable as it can be. They want to be able to support you through this change and addition to your family, but they can't do that if they don't know what you are thinking or feeling. They can't help you if you are lying to them either. I eventually realized through therapy that I wasn't being as forthcoming as I could have been either, something I wish I could go back and change.

There were so many opportunities for me to ask for help and I didn't take any of them. When I refer to asking for help, I'm not talking about asking someone to watch the baby while I go to the grocery store. The kind of help I needed was something much more substantial and reoccurring, although I can relate to those of you who are new mothers and have difficulty finding daycare. I quickly realized how hard it was to find someone to watch a newborn during the evening hours when I was working. Thankfully, with Dave having off every other weekend, I always made sure to work a double shift if I could, because not only was he around and able to be with Nathan, but it was free daycare. The hardest days for me, though, were Mondays and Tuesdays. I dreaded those days because I knew I would be home with Nathan by myself if I couldn't find a sitter. I would take him anywhere and everywhere, just so that there would be another person around me. We were rarely home alone together, and if we were, we were sleeping.

I thank the heavens above for blessing me with a child that would run errands with me all day long. Finn and Nadia, my two younger children, have an expiration time of two and a half hours. Once that time hits, they are finished, and they wanted to go home, but Nathan on the other hand was completely content bumming around. It isn't as though I thought I was going to hurt him or that I didn't trust myself, I just didn't want to be alone with him. I didn't really know what mothering a new baby looked like and I certainly didn't feel like how I thought mothers should feel. All I knew was that it was better if we were out shopping, or sitting at a friend's house, or having someone come over, than if we were left alone at the house together. I didn't know how I was going to feel, or if I was going to feel anything at all, but I knew I wasn't used to feeling the way I was feeling and I felt better, safer, just knowing someone else was with me. This should have been a red flag. I should have told someone this.

Although Mondays and Tuesdays weren't my best days, they also weren't always my worst. Occasionally, there would be a night when my mother had something going on and couldn't take Nathan, or my aunt would want a Friday off for a social gathering and I would have Nathan. There was one weekend night when Nathan was about a month old that sent me into a sheer panic. I didn't think that I could mentally or emotionally handle being alone with him, me being the sole provider of his care, even if it was only for eight hours while Dave was working.

At the time, my sister had been living with her best friend in an apartment close to where Dave worked and about 20 minutes from where Dave and I were currently living. I had called my sister and asked what she was doing and if she was home. I heard yes on the other end of the line and knew I was about 20 minutes from knocking on her door. I had Nathan's Pack n' Play in one hand, his diaper bag over my shoulder, and his car carrier on the other arm when I knocked on her door. She answered the door with a glass of red wine in one hand, country music playing the background, and her best friend standing in the living room slightly off in the distance. I handed her the car carrier and his things and said, "You need to watch him. Dave will pick him up after work or you can drop him off sometime tomorrow."

This is a moment I will never forget. I can hear the desperation as I type this sentence. She grabbed him and said, "OK." I set his things down in her living room, turned around, and walked down the hall toward the elevator. I can still vividly see the blueish-gray carpet leading back to the stainless steel elevators that would take me down to the parking lot where I could get into my car and finally feel relieved. My sister was 21, only a couple of years younger than I. She had no clue what was going on with me any more than I did, but when she shut the door behind her, she exchanged look of disbelief with her best friend. I am so appreciative of her support back then, and I know not everyone is as lucky as I was to have her in my corner.

Whether you are able to recognize it at the time or not, there are people in our lives whom we can talk to and rely on for help, whether it be a friend, a parent, a sibling, a nurse, a crisis hotline, or heck, even someone you know that is a mother themselves. I believe a part of me didn't want to acknowledge what I was going through, because it was a complete 180 degrees from everything I knew and understood. As if admitting my feelings and my mental state to myself or someone else would somehow mean that I was weak. I didn't want to feel like a failure. Motherhood is not a competition, and speaking up is one of the hardest and most honorable things you can do for yourself and your child, but it does mean that you have to actually speak up. You can't expect people to know what you are thinking and feeling if you don't say it out loud to someone else. I know that my sister would have taken Nathan regardless, but I also know that if I would have shared with her the severity of how I was feeling, she would have done more than just watch him that night. It took me a long time to talk to anyone about this, and even when I did, I didn't make it clear exactly what was going on with me.

A few months ago, I was talking with Anne, the mother of my stepchild, whom I have since become close to, even though our relationship together started out as anything but copacetic. She reminded me of a time when she had come to our house to pick up Tessa on an evening when Dave had to go into work for an extra mandated shift. She said she remembers stepping into the house from the front doorway while she waited for Tessa to grab her things. I was holding Nathan by the kitchen table, and she said I looked so empty, beat down, and defeated. Anne said she felt so sad for me in that moment and wished that she could have helped me in some way, but she didn't know how, given our turbulent relationship at the time. She didn't think it was her place.

Ironically, I remember exactly what day she had been talking about. Nathan had been only a few months old. I wanted to say something. I wanted to plead with her to not leave me alone, but I didn't. I was too scared she would use that against me somehow. I was scared for no real reason at all.

We often wonder if our relationship would have been different, or even better, if we would have both recognized what we saw in each other. She wishes she would have asked me if I was OK, and I wish she would have, too. That's not to say in that moment that I would have accepted her help, because my mind wasn't necessarily thinking clearly, but I think at the very least it would have planted the seed in my subconscious.

When I think about these moments, it brings me to tears. I am normally so strong and resilient. I have always done whatever needed to be done, whether I wanted to or not. I would finish whatever goal I set for myself, and when I set my mind to something, I always did it, so why couldn't I do just that? In my mind I constantly asked myself, "What is wrong with you? What are you doing? This is your child. Why don't you want to take care of him? You can do this, but if you think you can't or don't feel like you want to, why aren't you telling anyone? Why aren't you getting help?"

I like to believe that in my own way, I was telling my sister that I needed help—I just wasn't willing to admit it in so many words. Unfortunately, that did nobody any good. But it's not as if I sit here and blame someone else for me not asking for help. If I didn't even understand what was happening, how could I expect someone else to magically understand what I was going through? Sadly, it took me until Nathan was three and a half years old to understand what I had been through and slowly open up to the fact that I had postpartum depression.

Often times asking for help is one of the hardest things for people to do. If this is you, then you're not alone. Asking for help feels like you are surrendering control to someone else. It is in our nature to want to do things for ourselves, to have our independence, and asking for help can feel like you are giving up a part of that. We do not want to appear needy or like we can't manage the current situation.

If you feel like you are in over your head, the best thing to do is to put your pride aside and talk to someone. Let them help you figure out what it is that will help you. Just because you are asking for help does not mean that you are putting someone out or that you are a bother in any way. Most people want to help other people. The medical profession is full of people who want to help other people. These are people who literally make it their purpose in life to care for others when they are sick or unable to care for their loved ones themselves. It's rare to ask someone in your circle for help and they say no. If you find yourself in that situation, then reach out to someone else, whether that be another friend, a mental health hotline, your physician's office, or a local emergency room. Once you have gotten the help you need, reevaluate the relationship you have with the individual who said no.

What to take away from this chapter:

It is important to remember that people cannot read your mind. They might not necessarily know you're headed down a destructive path or that you are feeling sad and alone, but that doesn't mean they won't help you or that they don't want to help you. Everyone has bad days or hard days, and they might very well think this is a onetime occurrence, not necessarily understanding that this is what every day looks like for you.

It can hurt your ego to be painfully honest with yourself, but that doesn't mean you shouldn't do it. Doing so will allow you to verbalize your feelings to someone you trust. The sooner you are able to verbalize your feelings, the sooner you will begin your path to healing. Acknowledge how you are feeling to yourself and then go and tell someone.

CHAPTER FIVE

Trust Someone

When I was ten years old, my parents as well as my younger brother, sister, and I moved from a large metropolitan city to a small town 30 minutes north. In the winter of 1992, when the house was finally finished being built, we became official residents of a town with a little over 3,000 residents. I'm not entirely sure how, because this was before school choice was enacted, but my sister and I were enrolled as students in the district the summer prior to the start of the school year, even though we technically didn't live in the district yet. All I know is that it allowed us to avoid having to switch schools mid-year. For that, I was grateful. It's hard enough being the new kid, much less being the new kid who joins the class halfway through the year.

I was in the fourth grade and had mixed feelings about leaving the school I had attended previously. It was a cute school, and I have some fond memories, but I didn't have a ton of friends there—only a couple that I remember specifically. I know I was nervous about attending a new school that first day, but thankfully, those feelings were put to ease within minutes of taking my seat in my new classroom.

When the school year started that September, I had been assigned to Ms. Johnson's class. That's where I met Adrianne. I'm not sure if it was my all-black wardrobe that drew her to me or my sparkling personality, but whatever it was, I know the universe was doing me a favor that day. She had grown up in this tiny town, but never treated me like I was the new girl or an outsider. She was welcoming and nice to me from the very beginning. Ady made me feel like I belonged in the class just like the rest of the students, even though everyone else had gone to the same elementary school for the last several years and had known each other one way or another since kindergarten. I was especially thankful for someone I could sit next to at lunch, which was honestly the thing I was most nervous about! It wasn't long before we were having sleepovers at each other's houses every weekend. Her mother was even the council leader for our Girl Scout troop that met weekly, which meant more time with my bestie.

There are people in life that you just click with, and Ady was one of those people for me. We had become such close friends and so fast that it was difficult for anyone to believe we hadn't known each other our entire lives. It was as if we were old souls that knew each other in another lifetime.

That bond even got us into a little bit of hot water. Our teacher accused the two of us of cheating on an English test within the first few weeks of school that year. At the time, Ms. Johnson had arranged the desks in the classroom, so they formed several small circles. We didn't sit in the same circle, but our desks were within an arm's reach of each other. The specifics are a little hazy, but essentially, we had to write down words that described where we lived and places we visited, or something similar to that line of thinking. Don't hold me to it, but I think the test had to do with understanding nouns, verbs, adjectives, and things like that. Since we still didn't "technically" live in the district, my mom had warned me about elaborating on where our house was located until the building process was completed and we had moved in. Well, lo and behold, Ms. Johnson thought that was suspicious. She made us write letters to our parents labeling ourselves as cheaters and explaining in detail what happened and how we cheated. Ms. Johnson was even more irritated because neither Ady nor myself wavered as to why we had the same answers: it was just a coincidence.

When my mother picked me up from school that day, I told her what happened. I remember being absolutely pissed and can still picture where her minivan was parked. I stared at the water tower on the hill in the distance as I told her the story. It's funny how we can't always remember the words that someone said to us, but we can always remember how they made us feel. My mother was sympathetic, and she believed me, because it was obvious to her that this was one big accident. What really ate at my core though, even at 10 years old, was that someone who barely knew me was questioning my character and accusing me of something that I legitimately didn't do. I hate more than anything when people do that, and I have a really tough time moving past it. I hold on to that anger for way too long.

When I married my first husband, I knew within the first three months that the marriage was over, but I stayed married to him anyway. It was an incredibly stressful time, and I was deeply depressed. I'm talking lying in bed under the covers for days on end with the bedroom door closed and the curtains shut, locked away in complete darkness, only to come downstairs once in a while to lie on the couch and switch up the scenery. Often, the only glimmer of light that came from my room was a sporadic glare from the television that could be seen from under the door if you were walking by. I remember one time when I was lying in bed on a Saturday night, my usual routine, binge-watching *CSI* on my TiVo, when my husband at the time came home, three sheets to the wind, hoping to get me to come out to the bars with him and his friends. When I refused to leave with him, he ripped the covers off of me, grabbed the remote control out of my hands, and threw it as hard as he could against the wall. It broke into several pieces.

I will never forget that moment. Just writing this puts me in a full-on panic, because I can't forget how I felt and how I reacted. I started screaming and crying as I picked up the pieces to the remote control, trying to figure out how to put them back together again, saying, "What am I going to do now? Why would you do this to me? Why are you trying to hurt me?"

Aside from the obvious problems with this scenario, it was the first time that I realized I was deeply depressed and that I needed to talk to someone. The thought of not being able to use the remote control to watch my recorded television shows, my only sanctuary, was so devastating that I didn't think I could continue on. I didn't know how to make the depression I felt go away, and the only thing that helped was losing myself in a television show. I felt like I couldn't tell anyone the truth, because who marries someone, has this big, elaborate wedding, and then gets divorced three months later? (Other than Kim Kardashian, that is.) I was hurt, I was mad, and I was in a relationship with someone I didn't want to be with. I needed an excuse, and a good one, in order to justify a divorce, or so I thought at the time. I wasn't sure where my life was headed, nor how to fix it, and I didn't know how to relay those feelings.

About a year or so into that marriage, I got a tattoo on my ankle. One of my besties, Lori, whom I still am close with to this day, has the same tattoo on her knee. Her story resonated with me so much that I wanted the same tattoo, just bigger and more noticeable. I have several tattoos and they all represent a time in my life and what I was going through. This tattoo was a picture of my feelings toward life at that moment in time. I was married, depressed, and I didn't even know who I was anymore. Thankfully, I found the strength to walk away and say enough is enough, but if I hadn't met Dave, I probably would have stuck with it a little longer, even though that would have destroyed my mental health even more. The issue this represented, however, was that I hadn't dealt with any of the upsets from the first marriage before I got into a relationship with Dave. I then got pregnant and was about to be responsible for the care and well-being of another human.

Once I realized that the way I felt in general after Nathan was born was much different than the majority of other moms I knew, my confusion surrounding the entire postpartum experience only grew. I had experienced depression. I knew what that felt like. I had lived it. What was going on with me could not have been depression, because I didn't feel the same way I had felt when I was depressed prior. I couldn't put words to how I was feeling. I felt like no one would understand even if I explained it to them. I myself wasn't even sure how I was feeling or why I was feeling this way. It pains me to think that I didn't think I could turn to my parents or my family, my brother, or my best friends, but looking back, I was so worried that I would be such a disappointment that I just couldn't find the courage to say anything to anyone about how I was hurting. When you really get down to it, I just didn't trust sharing my emotions with anyone, because I thought they would minimize them or judge me, and it was something that I knew I just wouldn't be able to manage. I didn't want to feel like I was being questioned, that what I was telling them wasn't the truth.

As kids, we don't really understand learned behavior, but as adults it's easier to see how our past life experiences have molded us into the person we are today. After the birth of my daughter, Nadia, in the summer of 2016, I also suffered from postpartum depression. Through different forms of therapy and self-care, I was able to reflect back on my life and how much it hurt me when I realized someone didn't believe me when I was telling them the truth. It took me many years, many books, and lots of soul-searching to get to the root of the problem: I didn't tell anyone about my postpartum depression after having Nathan, because after I realized I wasn't well, I didn't think they would believe me, and even if they did, I didn't think they could do anything about it. It was easier to just keep quiet.

I didn't want to tell anyone that I was different, either. We spend so much of our life just trying to fit in, make friends, and be "normal." I didn't think anyone would really understand what it was that I wasn't exactly saying. I didn't want them to think that I couldn't take care of my child. I didn't want them to take Nathan away from me, but I also didn't want to take care of him even though I knew I had to. I wanted to feel the way I thought every other mother felt after they gave birth.

I didn't want anyone to think that I was mentally unstable, and I certainly didn't want them to say, "You'll feel better after you get some rest. It's hard with a new baby." I didn't want anyone to put words into my mouth or make assumptions about how I was feeling. I didn't want anyone to tell me to put the baby in a stroller and take a walk because fresh air and sun will make me feel better. Being outside has never made me feel better. I hate it when people tell me that because it doesn't work for me. I was scared someone was going to tell me to do something that wouldn't work and then I would feel even worse about myself than I already did.

After giving birth to Nadia and talking to someone, I was able to verbalize how I felt about certain situations and why I felt that way. I also learned how to look at what is happening in my life from another perspective, logically, removing some of the emotions.

When I think back to the situation with my fourth-grade teacher, it might seem silly to some, that something so insignificant would be so impactful, but for me it was. I no longer wanted to trust those in a position of authority, because they could say whatever they wanted, and it would be presented as facts. I was scared that someone would say something about the way I was feeling that wasn't true—that the story would get twisted, and not only would I have to live with my truth, but I would have to live with their lies, too.

When I think back on all these times in my life, it saddens me that I focused solely on the negative aspects. I missed something beautiful in the midst of it. At 10 years old, Ady showed me true friendship, but that isn't what I took away from the "cheating" scandal. She continued to show me how much she loved me each and every year we grew older. Her loyalty to me has never wavered. I am not entirely sure what I did to deserve her, but I do know that I would not be the person I am today without her. She had been there for me, by my side, whenever I needed her for the last 29 years. She was there for me each and every time my first husband wasn't. She saw me go through the destruction and devastation of that marriage. Why I didn't feel like I could talk to her about my lack of emotions and feelings after Nathan was born is a question without an answer to this day. All I can think is that my mind was playing tricks on me. Like many other women, I normally would rather talk about my feelings as opposed to staying quiet and closed off when something is bothering me. I wish I had trusted her enough to tell her what was really going on. I believe she would have convinced me to seek help, and I know she would have listened to me talk for hours if that is what I needed. I'm also fairly certain she would have told me that if I didn't feel comfortable talking to my doctor, then I needed to make an appointment with hers or that she would even go with me. Deep down, I knew that I could trust her to not think that I was a bad person or a bad mother. But why I couldn't bring myself to say anything to her sooner is a regret I think I will always have.

When I finally opened up to Ady, she beyond supportive and empathetic. It was difficult for her to put to words the way she had felt, because on one hand she was so proud of me for going back to work so early, only thinking of the physical part of childbirth. She couldn't believe how quickly I had "bounced" back and easy it was for me to get back into the swing of things. On the other hand, it was only after she had her daughter that she realized just how different our birthing stories had been. When I had visited Ady after Aubree was born, she noticed the look of unknown, loss almost, that spread across my face. The confusing look I had given her when I asked her why she was so happy caused a ripple effect. She was now confused because how else was she supposed to feel? It was then, and only then, that she realized just how different things were for us.

What to take away from this chapter:

Many times, in order for us to trust someone, they have to earn it. Once they earn that trust, however, they should be granted it. If you feel alone, or sad, or are not sure what you are feeling but think you might need help, you should talk to someone who has earned your trust. If they really care about you and your well-being, they will help you get help.

If you don't feel that you have someone you can trust, seek help from a medical professional regardless of the method of delivery. There are many health care providers that will see you and book a virtual visit as long as you have internet access.

If you are struggling emotionally, mentally, or physically, it's important to be aware of and understand how your past life experiences may have changed or are impacting your perspective on life or a particular situation. Our assumptions and reactions to particular situations might look quite different if we approach from a different angle or point of view. Additionally, it's important to remember that our feelings will differ drastically depending on our current frame of mind and emotional state.

CHAPTER SIX

Is Going to Work Self-Care?

I always remember my mother and father being working parents when I was growing up. Both of them were self-employed: My father owns a go-kart manufacturing company and my mother worked in direct sales. I didn't realize it until recently, but I always had a job where I picked which hours I worked. I may have had to punch a clock, but I was in control of what time my shift started.

My parents worked opposite shifts for most of my upbringing, my dad working day shift, my mother in the evenings. I remember them both being extremely diligent workers, but I tend to take after my mother. If my parents needed extra money, she worked extra hard to secure it. My parents did what they needed to do to support their children, and I respected that and still am very thankful I had the childhood I did.

I know I had it good compared to others. I knew a guy once who had parents that made him pay rent even though he was still in high school, and if he didn't write that check on the first Saturday of every month, they would threaten to kick him out. I was never subjected to that type of parenting, thankfully, and I appreciated that. I hope my kids will one day notice and be thankful for how hard I work to support them as well.

At almost 16 years old, I got a job working as a cashier at a local grocery store. I made around $60 to $75 a week, which doesn't seem like a lot, but to a teenager who didn't have any monetary commitments, it was more than enough. I lived in a town where you could drive around the perimeter of it and put maybe five miles on your vehicle. My job was close to home, and I wasn't far from school, so paying for gas at $1.01 a gallon was never an issue.

If there is one regret, I have in regards to money, it's that I wish I had been better at saving my money instead of spending it. When my stepdaughter was 17, we spent her entire senior year focusing on financing and budgeting, credit scores and credit cards. To this day, her mom thanks me for taking the time to help her with all that. She knows how to save appropriately, budget her expenses, and spend wisely. I didn't really have that with my parents, not that I blame them for that or anything. When I talked with my mom about it years later and asked her why, she said her dad was so tight and strict with money that she remembers her mom wearing the same eyeglasses for almost 20 years. My mom said that she never wanted someone else to tell her what to do with her money or tell her how to spend her money, so she didn't do that with her kids. I, on the other hand, could have benefited from some words of wisdom from my grandfather, because a 19-year-old with a $10,000 credit limit is not a clever idea. Sadly, I had to learn the hard way in order to teach that to my kids.

When I met Dave, we both were already starting out financially in the hole for several reasons. I knew that in order to pay off some of the debt we had and be able to give our unborn baby the standard of living that my parents gave me, I would have to work for it. My first year out of x-ray school, which was more than several years ago, I made just over $80,000, which is unheard of when you are 23-year-old new graduate. I worked my butt off, and just before Nathan was born, we were able to move out of our shitty little apartment and into a four-bedroom, two-bathroom side by side just a few miles away. The kids finally were able to have a backyard and Dave and I were able to afford a new mattress and kitchen table! It felt good.

The problem, though, was that it felt too good. I liked having the financial security that I hadn't in a long time. The little money my first husband and I made went to car payments and his bar tab. It wasn't ideal, to say the least, but I remembered how it felt when the car payment was due and we didn't have the money. I knew I never wanted to go back to that way of living.

I had gotten pregnant with Nathan only a few months after I graduated. I felt great during most of my pregnancy, other than the morning sickness. Thankfully, I was still able to work, a luxury I didn't have while pregnant with my second child. Often, I would put in 12- or 16-hour days, first working at a clothing store and then going to the hospital afterward. I also worked at a family restaurant on Friday evenings and Sunday mornings. I really was lucky that way, in that I felt good and could continue on with daily life as usual, because not all pregnancies go as smoothly. With Nathan, I was able to keep up at the same momentum I was pacing before I had gotten pregnant. Once Nathan was born, I assumed I would slow down, but that didn't happen.

The days after I gave birth to Nathan should have been some of the happiest of my life, filled with diaper changes, bottle feedings, snuggles, and cute photos. Those days should have been more than just days; they should have been a minimum of six weeks, if not the full 12 protected by law. Those days should have been a time filled with family and bonding. They should have been everything that most new mothers got to experience, but for me they weren't, and because they weren't, I went back to work. I relied on what I knew, the tried and true, to get me through one of the loneliest times of my life.

When it comes to caring for our own children, my husband and I currently have a good system in place, similar to what I remember my parents doing. Unfortunately, it took us years to get it to this point where we both feel like we value and respect the work each other does within our family. He has a schedule where he works seven days on, for 10-hour shifts, and then has the next seven days off. I tend to work more hours than he does, but he really maintains the home front. When I say he is amazing in that regard, I mean it. He vacuums, does the dishes, does the laundry, feeds the kids, gets the kids ready for school in the mornings, and takes care of maintenance on the cars. I tend to be the administrator behind the scenes, making sure we know what kid's activities are when and who has what appointment and when, plus how they are getting there, along with doing most of the mental work, paperwork, and errands that are needed when running a household.

It works for us, but that doesn't mean it came easily. It wasn't a routine that we fell into because we had a respectful conversation with each other one evening about how we wanted to run our household and raise our children. It was a model that was formed because Dave had to form it. He had to get the kids ready for the day. He had to make sure the kids got on the bus. He had to feed them and do house chores, because the reality was that I went to work and then I went to another job after that. I was at home to sleep and that's about it.

Being at home reminded to me that my life was not happening as I pictured it was going to. For me, being at home was harder than going to work, because at work I could forget about what it was I was and wasn't feeling. I knew how to work, and I knew what work expected of me. There, everything felt normal. I created an environment for myself that felt safe, and that environment consisted of punching a clock. I knew Nathan was in safe hands and being cared for. Getting involved with anything beyond that wasn't something for which I was mentally or emotionally prepared.

Since we didn't have a ton of money after Nathan was born, going to work felt like the smartest decision and the safest for me mentally. I thought I was fixing my mental health by leaving the environment that made me feel anxious, and I was making money at the same time. Sadly, though, this was not the best answer, and I was using work as a crutch instead of dealing with feelings and addressing them. Even worse, I used that crutch for years, and sometimes I still do when I get overwhelmed, although it pains me to admit. This was, and is, an extremely hard cycle to break because I made it my routine, and we all know once you start a routine and you get used to it, changing that practice can be extremely difficult.

When I had first had Nathan, the last thing Dave expected was to be raising a newborn baby mostly on his own. When Nathan was an infant, many of the bonding attributes that are normally recognized to the mother were something that Dave took on, simply because I wasn't around. I wasn't great at snuggling with Nathan, but I was good at taking pictures of Dave snuggling with Nathan. I didn't do skin-on-skin bonding with Nathan, but Dave did nearly every day until he was 10 months old. There were so many times that they were chest to chest, napping on the couch together. The number of pictures I have of Dave and Nathan spending quality time together is almost unbelievable. I have albums upon albums of the two of them, and that was before it was possible to take decent pictures on our phones. Many of those photos are of the things they were doing in the moment. Most of the photos I have of Nathan and myself back then are those that I took when we went somewhere, like the mall for a picture with Santa, or a friend's birthday party. Hardly any are of the day-to-day activities of raising my child.

After I had Nathan, I turned to my job and my career as an x-ray tech as a form of self-care, although that isn't really the correct use of the word. Although I may have thought I was doing what was best for my mental health, all I really did was turn my back to the problem. There was no working though my struggles to come through on the other side. There were no deep breaths, long walks, or meditation to help my mind and soul relax. Work was a tactic I used to avoid my problems instead of finding a way to fuel my body with healthy coping mechanisms. Work was high-stress trauma cases in a busy emergency room. It was anything but self-care.

When you are going through something like this, whether it's post-partum depression, another mental health crisis, or just the stressors of day-to-day living building up and weighing heavy on you, it's important that you maintain any and all of the healthy habits and self-care routines that you have used in the past that have worked for you. If you aren't sure what those items are, form a list of the things you like to do that calm your soul, clear your head, and bring you happiness. For me, one of the hardest things was accepting advice from others in regards to self-care, because it didn't work for me, and I felt like they were feeding me advice that didn't even have a placebo effect. If anything, it made them feel better, not me.

My advice is to go to your tried-and-true self-care routines. Do you have a favorite movie or television show you like to watch? Do you have a favorite scent? Can you light a candle and find a place where you can sit and journal or read a magazine, or book? Does exercise help? Can you go to the gym, go for a run, or take a barre class? Do you have a favorite playlist on Spotify or Apple Music you can listen to? Will a manicure or pedicure do the trick? Does volunteering or going to church or Bible study bring you peace?

I know it's easier to tell yourself to take some time for self-care than to actually do it, because for the first two years after Nathan was born, I certainly didn't follow the advice I am giving now. I avoided what I was going through at all costs instead of finding healthy alternatives to deal with my depression. I went to work when I should have gone to the doctor. I went to work when I should have gone to a therapy session. I went to work when I should have had family dinners. I went to work when I should have taken the kids to the park to play. I went to work when I should have found something to organize. I went to work when I should have watched *Fools Rush In*. I went to work when I should have listened to an audiobook. I went to work when I should have been resting. When anyone would ask, "Where's Chelsea?" the answer was always, "At work."

When we think about unhealthy habits, most of us don't think that going to work would be classified as such, but for me, work was the opiate of the masses. It was a source of contentment for me. I had watched my mother work hard to ensure I had the things I wanted as a teenager. I thought that I was doing a good thing by going back to work so soon, because I was able to provide my child with everything, I thought he needed in his life. I justified my actions to myself. Truth be told, he didn't need that Diaper Genie. He didn't need all those clothes. He didn't need all those toys, or entertainment devices. He needed love. He needed food. He needed sleep. He needed care and time.

I know there isn't anything I can do to go back and change my behavior, but I wish I could. I wish that I would have said to someone that I needed help, or at least started to talk about what it was that I did need so that I could take better care of myself and loved ones. I didn't feel like I was bonded with my child in the way I thought I would be. I didn't feel much of anything. I didn't even know who I was or what I wanted, so it was easier to go work. I am not naive in that I think everything would have been perfect if I didn't have postpartum depression, because I don't think that's reality either, but I most definitely know it could have looked different if I would have gotten help sooner and realized what self-care actually meant. I am not suggesting that it would've been easy for me or that it will be easy for you. I regret my decision to keep quiet about my depression and I wish I had more time with Nathan when he was a baby. I missed so much. I know that I likely would have been put on some medication sooner than I was and been submerged in therapy. I know that it might have taken months before I started to see a change in my feelings, mood, or behaviors, but months would have been better than years.

What to take away from this chapter:

Everyone uses coping mechanisms to find comfort during a stressful time, but it's important that they are healthy coping skills. Falling back on something that is comfortable doesn't necessarily mean that is the best choice. There are thousands of peer-reviewed articles by staff and physicians that offer advice for finding beneficial coping mechanisms to get you through a tough time. Start there if you are unsure where to look. Your own physician or mental health counselor can also offer information when you need it.

Form positive habits in life that you can conduct through the good times and the bad. Our habits will offer comfort when we are struggling. This means that the healthy habits you form now could be beneficial to you in the future if you at some point find yourself in a trying time. If you are currently using habits that are risky to your health in everyday life, alter that course now so you don't continue to use these habits when you find yourself stressed. Otherwise, it will only make it more difficult to walk away from those unhealthy habits in the future.

Self-care comes in three forms: physical, mental, and emotional well-being. It is important to have a healthy balance of the three. Finding what works for you will be essential to your welfare as you go through life. It will look different for each and every one of us and that's OK. It might mean a long walk on a trail near your house, it might be taking a yoga class once or twice a week. It might be watching your favorite show on re-run as you scroll through Instagram. It might be journaling or going out to dinner with your friends. Whatever it might be, self-care is best when you choose what works for you.

CHAPTER SEVEN

A Glimmer of Light

During the time I was pregnant with Nathan, I wasn't overly concerned about finding daycare coverage for when Dave and I were working, but the thought had been floating around in the back of my mind. Although we both worked second shift, I had the ability to change the shift I worked if I wanted to or needed to. I also had the ability to pick which days of the week I wanted to work, and I only needed to give my availability a few weeks before the schedule was posted. In that respect, working in radiology is a great field for parents, because hospitals need coverage 24/7/365. Even if you were to take a clinic job somewhere, with urgent care centers being open as late as 10:00 p.m., and only closed on national holidays, there were still many opportunities to flex your hours. As I had more children, I was even more grateful for the plasticity. While I was pregnant, I had planned on being off of work for about eight to 12 weeks, and so I would secure a daycare provider during that time. After one week postpartum, I realized I was going to be in a predicament quickly if I didn't find someone to watch Nathan for a good part of the day.

I joined a group on Facebook whose sole purpose was to connect those who needed childcare with those who were willing to provide it. I lived for this group. I finally found someone who ran an in-home daycare about 12 minutes from where I lived. As an added benefit, it was on my way to and from work. I was so relieved that I finally found someone. However, once I actually called her, I found out that not only was she full, but she only provided care until 6:00 p.m. This was a problem for me, because I took the lead technologist position, which was from 1:00 p.m. until 9:00 p.m., and I still had about a 25-minute drive to get to her house from my workplace.

I was devastated and started to really panic. I believe wholeheartedly that the universe knew I needed a door to open, which led me to Heather.

Heather was a blessing from the minute I met her and meeting her was nothing short of a gift from God. There are not enough words in the English language to describe what this woman did for me. When I gave her a call to set up a time to meet her, she made sure that I was looking for something she could provide. She was very thorough, and as it turned out, the childcare I needed did align with what she could provide, so we arranged to meet the following week at her place. At this point Nathan was just a few weeks old.

The first time I drove up to her apartment, I was not overly impressed with the building, and I was surprised she could run a successful daycare in such a small place. I was quickly proved wrong. When I stepped into her home, she was clearly devoted to the children she cared for. She had absolutely everything that a child could need or want in such a small space. She used the bedrooms effectively and efficiently for nap time and for a changing space. Her kitchen was organized with all the supplies that a child would use to feed themselves. She had high chairs and booster seats and a big table for arts and crafts. She knew how to multitask a space better than I have ever seen before. She had books beyond books for the kids and toys put away in storage totes throughout her living room. The walls were covered with pictures of her daughter from the minute she was born through present time. She was stuffed to the brim with children's things, but she was organized and knew where everything was.

Once Nathan and I took a seat in her living room on the red couch, Heather told me a little bit about her background, and I shared mine. As *Mickey Mouse Clubhouse* played softly on the television, she told me her expectations and asked if that was something I could respect. We discussed the hours I needed, and thankfully she was able to work with them. She also handed me a sheet of references that I could call. I'll admit, I took the sheet knowing full well, I was never going to call those references. I had already heard and seen enough. She could watch Nathan until 9:30 p.m. and she seemed responsible; after all, she was caring for two other children besides her own, and they all were well taken care of from what I could see. I asked her how long until Nathan could start attending regularly. That was the one and only question I had for her. She responded that since she was state certified, legally she could not take Nathan until he was six weeks old. My heart sank, but I said okay, I would be in touch, and then I left. The next day, I set up a schedule with Heather over the phone for Nathan's first week.

The day finally came. Six weeks had passed since I gave birth, and Nathan was able to attend his first day at daycare. At 12:30 p.m., I carried him in his navy-blue infant carrier up to Heather's apartment. I entered long enough to hand her my child and his diaper bag, said I would be back at 9:30 p.m. to pick him up, and then I left. I don't remember if I said goodbye to him, but I'm fairly sure I didn't. I know for certain I didn't cry. I'm certain I came across as a stone-cold bitch, for lack of a better word. I got in my car and drove off as if it was a normal day and I hadn't just given my newborn baby to a woman I had known for seven minutes. While I drove to work, it never even concerned me that I had handed off my baby to someone whose references I didn't even bother to check.

When I say that Heather was a gift from God, I mean it. She loved Nathan like her own. She had a three-year-old herself, and if you didn't know any better, you would have thought Nathan was hers too. I never talked to her about my struggles with postpartum depression, but she must have known I was struggling, because there were so many times when she went out of her way to help me. At the end of a long week watching everyone else's children while their parents were at work, she would offer to keep Nathan longer than she was supposed to. She would occasionally call me at work and say Nathan fell asleep early, that if I wanted to pick him up around 9:00 in the morning instead of that night, it was fine with her. I hate to admit it, but those nights were some of my favorites.

I got lucky when I found Heather, and there isn't day that goes by that I am not appreciative. Taking your child to daycare can be such a scary and anxiety-filled experience for many people. You pray that you are able to put your trust in another human to care for your most precious possession while you are at work, but there is always that question that lives rent-free in your mind: What if something happens? I know that there are tons of parents who take their child to daycare, knowing they are completely safe and adored, but you also hear of parents who trusted their child with the wrong person and now live their worst nightmare each day because something terrible happened. I am blessed that I was not in the latter category.

When someone is going through postpartum depression, they aren't necessarily thinking as clearly as they might have prior to the depression. Right now, I can honestly say that the thought of me handing over my child to someone I barely know is enough to make me sick to my stomach. Not only does the thought of it make me sad, but it also was an extremely risky decision to act on. If Heather hadn't been the respectable, professional, and loving daycare provider that she presented herself to be, I can't imagine the insurmountable guilt I would be living with today if something would have happened while Nathan was under her care. I thank God that I didn't subject him to someone who could have abused him mentally, emotionally, or physically.

Even though we might struggle to understand it, I believe God has a plan for us. Whether you interchange God with a higher power, the universe, or nothing at all, I also believe that when it comes to religion, there are so many different faiths that can coexist in our world today. I have heard many people say, "If God exists then why do terrible things still happen on earth?" Or, "If God exists, then why did you have postpartum depression, or why does mental illness exist in the first place?" The fact is, we all have the ability to make our own decisions, and He gave us that ability. We unfortunately don't always make the best decisions, and at times must deal with the ramifications of those decisions. Even if you don't pray to God, how many times have you said to the open sky, "Please let get that job I interviewed for," or "Please let my kids come home safely"? How many times have you said, "Please God, if you just ... then I will ..."?

In regard to my postpartum depression, I knew I didn't feel right, but I didn't get any help either. I made that decision to ignore how I was feeling instead of choosing to address it head-on. Thankfully, it is clear to me now that sometimes we have to go through difficult journeys in life to experience our own personal growth. Going through these inconvenient situations in our life can seem unbearable at times, but rising out of trials often gives us compassion for others and the ability to empathize with them. It's usually the tough times when people step up and show great acts of kindness.

Sometimes we find ourselves asking, "Why, God?" I ask myself the same thing on a pretty regular basis, especially when I start thinking about the years since I had children. The truth is, if I hadn't experienced postpartum depression, I would have never met Heather, whom I honestly believe tutored my son more than I ever could have those first three years of his life. She did things with him and taught him things I never would have. If I hadn't experienced postpartum depression, I would have never read about Andrea Yates or any of the other woman who struggled even more than I did. I would have never authored this book. I would have kept all of this a secret between my husband and I, and I would have never shared my story. My children would have never known what I had gone through. It would have been something no one ever spoke of. But now, I am able to share my experience and help my sons understand something their partner may or may not experience after giving birth, should they choose to have children. I believe this will help them have compassion and understanding. I also want to be able to explain this to my daughter one day, as she has a higher chance of experiencing this, given the family history.

What to take away from this chapter:

You will go through challenging times in your life, in your pregnancy, in your marriage, or at some other point during your time here on earth. You will get through it, maybe not today, maybe not tomorrow, but eventually. Rely on your faith or spirituality to help you. Lean on God or your church family for support. There is a bigger picture than just this moment in time. *If you are an atheist, is there something else you are drawn to that can help you get through this time? Does the universe have a bigger plan?*

Find something to be thankful for. Find something positive about each day to remind yourself that life is a blessing, *and you are fortunate to be present. Like Alice Morse Earle once said, "Every day may not be good ... but there's something good in every day." Find a positive quote on the internet with a simple google search and try to apply that quote to your life. Turn a negative experience into a positive experience and rewrite the ending. For example, I could have said I had postpartum depression after I gave birth to two of my children and left it at that, feeling sorry for myself that I didn't have the joyous experience other mothers did after they gave birth, but instead, I chose to find the positive in it. If I hadn't had this diagnosis, I would not have met a wonderful woman, who not only cared for my son, but also cared enough about me to help me when I needed it. If I hadn't had this diagnosis, I would not be able to share my story about how I got through it.*

CHAPTER EIGHT

Later Pregnancies

For most of this book, I have talked about the postpartum depression I developed after I delivered Nathan, my first-born son. I have three biological children: Finn, my second-born son, whom is almost five years younger than Nathan, and Nadia, my daughter, who is four years younger than Finn. Although I had an extremely difficult pregnancy with Finn, I was fortunate that I didn't experience postpartum depression after he was born. Just because I had it once didn't guarantee that I would have it again, although my chances were elevated.

After I gave birth to Finn, I experienced what I imagine the 85 percent of women who don't have postpartum depression experience after giving birth. To put it simply, I was so happy. I loved every minute of my time with him when he was a baby and cherished every moment. When Finn was born, I had just upgraded to the newest iPhone and was using it extensively to take pictures, as opposed to the common digital cameras that were popular before that. I have this one photo stored in the cloud that I took when Finn was about two months old. The sun is starting to creep through the windows, and it is about 5:30 in the morning. Finn is smiling as he lies on my lap in his blue onesie.

When I took that picture that morning, which in and of itself was a feat since I absolutely hate mornings, I was so joyful. I can replay that day in my mind at any given moment and remember exactly how I felt: elated jubilation. I was so fortunate just to be in that moment with him. He stared at me with such love. For a night owl like myself, it was extremely out of character for me to be so pleasant and eager to start the day so early in the morning. It still shocks me, but the best part about the whole thing was that I wasn't only delighted to be sitting there with my son, but I was also so thankful. I knew that this time postpartum was going to be different from what I experienced after Nathan. I could feel it.

When I found out I was pregnant with Finn, Dave and I were just starting to get back on track as a married couple. The postpartum depression I had after Nathan and my inability to address it had done a real number on our marriage. Because of that, this time around, Dave came with me to several doctor's appointments. (Dave didn't come to any appointments with me when I was pregnant with Nathan, even though it was our first child together, and although it was hurtful at the time, I can recognize that we weren't necessarily in the greatest place together either. And although he may not have showed up for the doctor's appointments, he certainly stepped up after Nathan was born.) When it was time to have a discussion with the physician after she had examined me, Dave wanted the opportunity to ask a question: "What can she do so she won't go nuts after this pregnancy?" That was the one and only question he had, and he fully expected it to be answered.

Aside from the fact that this question is anything but politically correct, there isn't necessarily something you can or cannot do to ensure that you don't get postpartum depression. There isn't a magic pill you can take, although the three of us decided that I would go on an antidepressant throughout the pregnancy, and it would gradually increase in potency the last month of the pregnancy. Since I wasn't going to breastfeed, there were a plethora of other options for after delivery, should I need them. Having already experienced depression in my pre-pregnancy days, as well as postpartum depression, it was going to be much easier for not only myself but also my spouse to recognize the signs this time around.

Since I had gone back to work so soon after Nathan was born, and this time felt so different, I was in no hurry to get back after delivering Finn, even though I was working as the lead x-ray technologist during the day, a position that I absolutely loved. I had an amazing team of individuals working with me back then, and they were so supportive and accepting of my situation. Even though I missed collaborating with my team and having a full-time income, I still was not in a hurry to punch the clock day in and day out, so I decided to take the full 12 weeks off after Finn was born.

I was enjoying staying at home with him so much that when the time came to go back full-time, I wasn't ready. I could not imagine spending a few hours away from Finn, much less a full nine with the commute. I know that what I was feeling was not postpartum anxiety, because I had no problem leaving Finn from time to time to go to the store or to visit with a friend. I knew he was being taken care of and I knew that I wouldn't be gone long.

By the time Finn was seven months old, I just couldn't take it anymore. I didn't want to work full-time. I felt like I was missing so much, and since I hadn't experienced any of this before, I decided to step down from my position as the lead radiology technologist and only work part-time. I didn't care what I would have to do, or what spending cuts I was going to have to make. I was not going to continue to work full-time and be away from him all day for several days in a row. This was such a drastically different feeling from when I had Nathan that I didn't want to miss the opportunity to spend time with him and watch him go through all of baby's "firsts." I had no idea how long I would feel like this or how long I would want to continue to stay with him, but I knew that if it was a possibility, then it was an opportunity I was going to take. For the first time, I was present, and there was nowhere else I wanted to be than with my baby.

When Finn turned three and a half years old, I went back to work full-time, working third shift. I would work for seven days in a row, 10-hour days, and then I would have off for seven days in a row. This is a popular shift for staff who work in hospitals, especially larger facilities, where burnout can easily occur. By this time, Finn was getting closer to four years old, and I knew that he would be going to school shortly for a good part of the day. This allowed me to be home with him more days than not, and I would be sleeping when he was in school. It also worked well because Dave was working the other 7/70 shift at the hospital on nights, which meant that he would work when I was off, and I would work when he was off. It was a little tricky finding that balance for Dave and me to spend quality time together, because when I was off, he was working, and when he was off, I was working, but it was a sacrifice I was willing to make to be able to earn a full-time paycheck and still be home with Finn. Even though I was going back to work, I still wasn't ready to give up my time with him. I had spent the last three years being by his side, and he was my baby.

Finn and I had created a bond that I hadn't had the opportunity to form with Nathan until he was much older. It is something that still crosses my mind and saddens me when I think about it. I wish that I had gotten help for the postpartum depression with Nathan years before I actually did. I feel I got cheated out of that special time with him. In some aspects, Nathan was lucky: he spent time socializing with other kids, giving him opportunities that Finn never got. Nathan had so many more experiences. One of my favorite things to look back on are all the art projects Nathan made when he was at Heather's, and all the pictures she took of him learning to socialize with his peers at such an early age. It saddens me, though, knowing that he spent so much time away from me.

As for Finn, he was at home with me, and only me. Sure, he had siblings, but they were years older and in school most the day. Finn was light-years behind Nathan in that respect. He didn't really start talking until he was three years old, and even once he did start talking, no one knew what he was saying except me. It was almost as if we had our own language. He went everywhere I went. He snuggled and slept with me seven nights a week while Dave was at work. He was an extension of me.

We weren't able to put Finn into four-year-old kindergarten until half-way through the school year, because he didn't communicate like others his age, even though I knew exactly what he was saying when he said it. Nathan, however, was able to count to fifteen and write most of his ABCs as well as use scissors effectively by the first day of 4K. He was so advanced for his age. I am grateful that with the help of an IEP (individual education plan), Finn was able to catch up to his peers.

Sometimes I have to step back and look at the picture as a whole. There were positives and negatives with both scenarios, and I am most grateful that all my children were born healthy and happy. For the longest time, I felt so guilty for being able to have that bond with Finn that I didn't have with Nathan, and on the same hand, I felt guilty for having Finn stay home with me, because maybe I was doing him a disservice. Was he behind his peers because I didn't do enough to teach him things? Was he behind because of the antidepressants I took while pregnant? I felt like I had picked one child over the other because I had not connected with Nathan the way I had with Finn. It was really something difficult to wrap my head around.

I know that parents aren't supposed to have favorites, and plenty of people reminded me of that, but for the longest time, I felt like Finn was my favorite. What it really came down to, though, was that I spent more time with him. The grass was greener because I watered it. I knew his personality better. I was investing in that relationship day in and day out. We created memories together that I didn't create with Nathan. To put it simply, I didn't put in the time with Nathan that I did with Finn.

By the time my postpartum depression started to get better after Nathan was born, he was already a couple of years old. Once I realized that what I had with Finn was something that I missed with Nathan, I made sure to dedicate special time with him to make up for what I lost in the beginning. I made sure to create that bond with Nathan, even if I was off to a late start. I'm grateful for the relationship we have today, and I see so much of myself in him. This helped greatly as I started to get to know who he was. Finn's personality is so different from mine that if I wouldn't have given birth to him, I would wonder how I could be his mother. He is silly, loves to make people laugh, and everyone he talks to leaves with a smile on their face.

I am so glad I was able to experience the feelings and emotions after giving birth to Finn that I didn't get the opportunity to experience with Nathan, at no fault of anyone's. By having Finn, I knew what I was missing with Nathan. It also helped me understand I would have to find peace with that somehow, because if not, the guilt would probably eat at my heart.

What to take away from this chapter:

Postpartum depression isn't something that every mother will experience, nor is it something that is guaranteed if you had it with a prior pregnancy. Additionally, just because you didn't have it with your first pregnancy doesn't mean you won't get it with a later pregnancy. It is a condition to be mindful of, so that you can get the help you need if you have it, but it isn't something that you should necessarily worry about unless you start to have symptoms.

If you are not able to bond with your baby due to the fact that you had postpartum depression, it doesn't mean all hope is lost or that you don't love your child or that you didn't want to form that bond. I didn't form a strong bond with Nathan until years later, and my relationship with him is the one I am most proud of. I think of how far we have come together and how much I love and respect him. I would absolutely do anything for him and will protect him at all costs.

Just because you felt one way at one point in your life does not mean that you will feel that way one month later, one year later, or even a decade later. People change, people evolve, and people can get past certain traumas in their lives and move forward, stronger than when they started.

CHAPTER NINE

Mommy Guilt

Mommy guilt is a real thing. I talked a little bit about it in the last chapter, but mommy guilt can also mean other things and come in other forms. I felt guilty because I had postpartum depression with one child but didn't with the other, but some mothers might experience that guilty feeling on a different scale.

I have heard some moms say that when they leave the house and don't take their kids with them, they feel a pit in their stomach. Some mothers experience it on date night when they leave their child with the babysitter, even if it is only for a couple of hours. Other moms experience mommy guilt when they go back to work, and some experience it when they work too much. I read about moms who feel guilty if they can't breastfeed their child. Some mothers experience mommy guilt and aren't even sure why.

Mommy guilt comes in many fashions, and it certainly doesn't discriminate. It can also come out of the clear blue sky. I hear working moms say they have mommy guilt after scrolling through Instagram on their lunch break and seeing that cute project Susie made with her daughter an hour ago, while their child is in daycare. I hear stay-at-home moms say they have mommy guilt because their child can't cope when they leave the room. Their children have full-on anxiety attacks because they are so used to being side by side with their mom all day and night that the sheer absence of them, even if only for a minute, is too much to bear. Some moms have guilt because they let their kids eat too many sweets, some moms have guilt because they don't monitor how much screen time their children have, and some moms have guilt because they have two weeks of laundry waiting to be washed, folded, and put away. Mommy guilt is everywhere, and it comes in all shapes and sizes.

During the years that I had postpartum depression, I don't remember having this guilt I am speaking of, although after processing what I went through many years later, the guilt hit me hardcore. My husband Dave, for many years, much later in our relationship, would try to comfort me by saying, "They will never find out. They don't have to know you had postpartum. They won't remember, and I'm certainly not going to tell them." Although his intentions were good, those comments didn't necessarily make me feel better, nor did it take my feelings of guilt away.

Often, this parent guilt is classified as a feeling of not doing the "right" thing for your child and can turn into a fear that you are going to "mess up" your child if you make the wrong decision(s). The worst part about this guilty feeling is that it might be temporary or it might be something that lasts longer. You have to make a conscious decision every day to prevent it from consuming your mind, body, and soul. For me, most of the time my guilt surrounded the fact that I was never home, and I didn't have that bond with my child that I knew other mothers had with theirs. I was hardly ever with Nathan for an extended period of time, unless we were both sleeping. I wasn't spending quality time with my child the way my husband was. The thought of spending time at home caring for my child brought me zero joy. It was absolutely terrifying. Everyone was better off, or so I thought.

We have all heard the phrase, "You can't take care of someone else if you aren't taking care of yourself first." It's the number one reason flight attendants tell you to put on your own oxygen mask before you help others in the event the airplane is going down. You won't be able to help someone else if you yourself have passed out due to a lack of oxygen. The same principle applies when it comes to mommy guilt. If you notice that these feelings are creating an abnormal amount of anxiety and stress for you, speak up to your health care professional. It could be postpartum anxiety or postpartum depression that hasn't been addressed. Mommy guilt does not make you a bad mother, but if it gets in the way of you being able to care for and support your baby, then there is a bigger issue that needs to be confronted and that's important to take notice of and then act on.

I myself struggle with mommy guilt on occasion even to this day, and I wonder if it will ever truly go away. Once I started to address the postpartum depression and all the events that took place during that time, the guilt had really sunk in. I still am learning to manage my thoughts and find ways to cope with them when they creep up. Thankfully, though, most of the time, I get better each day at recognizing that I am doing the absolute best I can for my kids, even though it might not look perfect.

When Nathan was younger, I simply wasn't around. I was working 12-to-16-hour days, and then would be awake for a couple of hours before falling asleep the rest of the time. By the time I realized what I was doing, I had created a habit that can only be defined as being a workaholic; a habit that is extremely hard to break. I didn't have the mommy guilt back then because I couldn't see past the bleak existence that I had been living in to even take notice. I thought that working all the time and allowing anyone to take care of my child as long as it wasn't me was doing what was best for my family. It took me years to acknowledge I had postpartum depression, and once I had, the mommy guilt hit me like a Mack truck. What kind of mother chooses work over her kids? That is essentially what I felt like I had done for many years. I know many people say it isn't about how much time you spend with your child, but rather the quality time you spend with your child. Frankly, I wasn't doing either.

It is amazing how you can convince yourself you are a terrible person just by the way you talk about yourself, which is even more proof that positive affirmations should be done daily. I was absolutely disgusted by my behavior, and once I recognized what was going on with me, I thought it was too late. The days, weeks, months, and years had gone by. Nathan was two years old by the time I slowly started to work through the depression. Once I started to feel like I had returned to a somewhat normal baseline for myself, I didn't know how to deal with those feelings, so I let them aggravate me for way too long—something I do not recommend. It wasn't until Nathan was six years old that I was really able to forgive myself for all that time I missed with him.

When Nathan was about three and a half years old, I got pregnant with Finnian, and I was forced to stop working after being put on bed rest a few months into the second trimester. I had torn my placenta after carrying Christmas boxes up and down the stairs to put into storage after the holiday season was over. Looking back, I now see this as a blessing in disguise, because I was forced to slow down. Make no mistake though, taking things at a slower pace wasn't a decision that I made on my own, nor one I was happy about.

This is another one of those situations where I can see the positive aspect now that I have moved past that time in my life. During my pregnancy with Finn, I was on bed rest for six weeks, and then was allowed to be on my feet for only so many hours a day, with many restrictions in place after that. I had to do this not only to care for my own body, but for my unborn baby as well. I didn't want to lose the pregnancy and I knew that I needed to follow the doctor's orders, which meant that when she said bed rest, she meant it. I could get off the couch or recliner long enough to go to the bathroom and take 10 minutes to shower. I knew that if I overexerted myself, causing a loss of that pregnancy, the mommy guilt would haunt me for many, many years, all because I had to hurry up and put the Christmas decorations away. I remember telling myself that if I followed doctor's orders and still lost the baby, then at least I did my absolute best to protect us both. It was my own way of addressing mommy guilt before I even had mommy guilt to address.

Think about how many times you might give yourself a pep talk before you do something or try to rationalize a decision you are making just to ease those nagging thoughts. How many times do we overthink a scenario and rationalize what we are doing or the decision we are making even when we know we are making the best decision? If feeling guilty wasn't a normal emotion, would we ever second-guess our choices? Thankfully, I was able to carry Finn to full term and he was born healthy, meaning I didn't have to live with any guilt, but I do sometimes wonder: if I hadn't been in such a hurry to put away those Christmas decorations, would any of that even happened?

One of the best ways to overcome that nagging feeling of mommy guilt is to find where that guilt is stemming from. I don't always love therapy, particularly if I feel like the counselor is judging me, which I often feel like they are (although I am told that usually is not the case and that is just my perception of the encounter). Despite this, when you have someone, you can talk to who can help you understand your motivations behind a behavior, a lot of comfort can result. I don't regularly go to therapy anymore and haven't seen a therapist since my postpartum diagnosis with Nadia, but one thing that I did really love was that I was able to talk to someone who helped me figure out why I thought the way I did. Our thoughts are our thoughts, and our feelings are our feelings. It is challenging work when you have to redirect your decisions, actions, and behaviors because of what you feel in the moment. Your emotions can cause you to act in a way that might not be the way you would have normally managed a situation. Emotions can be hard to control, but it's important to remove your emotions from the equation and think rationally about the problem or issue without acting on it at once. I found that if I could understand why I behave or think a particular way or why it was that I thought a particular way, I could make a conscious decision to work through those feelings and change my course of action or reaction when proper.

During the time that I had postpartum depression with Nathan and Nadia, I made decisions that I wholeheartedly regret. I acted on my feelings and my emotions in the moment, and I had no idea that I was basing my actions and making decisions on these spur-of-the-moment feelings, especially after Nadia was born. I wouldn't sleep for days on end, and then when I would sleep, I would be out for days on end. The disrupted sleep certainly didn't help in terms of thinking clearly and let me say this: making decisions that will affect your entire family after not sleeping for days on end is one of the worst things you can possibly do. The guilt I had to live with for many years after that was torturous. Trust me when I say that acting on a decision you made because of how you felt after not sleeping for days won't be in your best judgement.

Whether you feel a small amount of mommy guilt, or a larger load is still significant. Is there a reason you feel guilty? Are you working second shift and blaming yourself because you can't read your child a book before bed and tuck them in at night? Are you working during business hours and therefore cannot volunteer in your child's classroom or attend field trips? Do you feel guilty because your kids, or even you yourself, spend too much time on electronic devices? Identify the source of the guilt. Once you have found it, write it down somewhere. Then write down an action plan to change that behavior, and start small. I repeat myself here: start small. Grand gestures are great and all, but if you're looking to make a real change to something that potentially has been bothering you for years, the likelihood of you succeeding is better if you can make one or two changes at a time rather than jumping full force ahead. I still use this process today, even though my depression has subsided.

My youngest, Nadia, is five years old. She spends too much of her time making TikToks or playing Roblox on iPad. I hate how much time she spends on electronics right before bed. In fact, I hate how much time all my kids spend on electronics, especially as they get older. I know limiting screen time is important and the blue light affects your sleep, but I didn't know where to start. I felt so guilty for letting them spend so much of their time on electronics, but I also felt as though I wasn't in a position to change that, since I worked second shift most nights of the week. If I wasn't around to check their screen time or regulate the amount of time spent on electronics, how was I ever going to change that behavior?

It really was counterproductive thinking, because ultimately, I always gave up, thinking it was too large of a task to take on. In order to overcome this, I had to get to the route of why my daughter being on her phone the last half hour before bed bothered me so much. When I broke it down to the simplest form, it was because I hated that I didn't have a bedtime routine with her. I heard so many of my other mommy friends talk about their bedtime routines for their kids, but I couldn't provide that for mine. The guilt I felt about not being able to give my daughter a hug goodnight before she went to bed made it that much harder for me to take away the bedtime routine that she created for herself, i.e., watching TikToks and playing Roblox on her iPad. Deep down, I didn't want to take this away from her, because I didn't think I had a practical alternative.

That being said, I knew what was triggering my mommy guilt: another mom being able to do something with their child that I thought I was missing with mine. From there, I was able to address my feelings head-on and do something about it. If I wasn't able to change my work schedule to be there at bedtime, I could make small adaptations to ease my feelings. I could FaceTime her before bed each night. I could create a time that was special to the two of us earlier in the day to form our own bonding moments. Additionally, just being able to understand why something bothered me made a world of difference. It gave me a sense of insight and I was able to move past the topic without giving it laser focus. I was no longer going to allow it to live rent-free in my mind.

We all value different things. Some of us value quality time. Some of us value friends and family. Some of us value kindness and volunteering. Some of us value objects of sentimental value and some of us value them all. For me personally, I place value on love and happiness and being a productive member of society. If my kids are happy and contributing to society in a positive way, then I am satisfied as a parent. Maybe my kids don't have a mom who can tuck them in at night before bed, but they have a mom who makes sure they get their homework done. Maybe my kids don't have a mom who limits how much time they spend on their electronic devices at night, but they have a mom who has them engaged in other activities that don't involve a computer or iPad. I figured out what it is that I want most for my children, what it is that I value and hope to instill in them, what it is that will make me proud of the way I am raising my children, and I try to redirect my guilt into a new way of thinking. I'm not claiming that this is the answer for everyone, but I know that changing the way I viewed my situation, changing my perspective of things, and understanding why I was feeling one way versus another has helped me tremendously. Sometimes we must reevaluate our position or change the way we are looking at a situation to overcome those feelings and move forward.

Another way to address the mommy guilt is to surround yourself with people who will support you and uplift you. Feeling guilty is a normal human reaction. Most mothers have mommy guilt in one way or another. If you talk to another mom whom you have a good relationship with and can be honest and open with, there is likely a good chance that after you share your feelings with her, she will help you identify other areas where you excel as a mother. Surround yourself with those people who want to support you as opposed to surrounding yourself with individuals who only add to your mommy guilt.

Take, for example, my relationship with Anne, my stepchild's biological mother. I often share with her the many ways I am failing as a mother, and she turns right back around and points out other ways in which I excel. When I say, "I'm so busy working and going to school that I miss the trivial things," she says, "I'm proud of you. You are showing your kids how to work hard and go after what they want in life. It won't always be this way. This is only temporary." She redirects the guilt I am feeling into something positive and reminds me that this isn't forever, it's a temporary problem and an ending is near. If she would have instead said, "Man, that sucks. When Tessa was her age, I was able to read her a book every night and snuggle with her on the couch with a bowl of ice cream for a nighttime treat," I would feel worse about my situation. If that were the case, it might be best to rethink surrounding myself with her company, or at the very least limit discussions with her to something more platonic. She wouldn't be contributing anything positive to the conversation in this situation. If she is a good friend or confidant, she will know what it is you value and supply a judgement-free and supportive ear. If you don't have anyone who you think can do that for you, then your next best choice is to find a neutral party to confide in, like a therapist or counselor, or even a support group. A good friend can sometimes be hard to come by but starting out in a support group with individuals who have things in common with you is a good place to start.

What to take away from this chapter:

Most women have some sort of mommy guilt. It is quite common and something that almost everyone struggles with at one time or another. Finding the right support group or talking to someone who has an unbiased opinion will help you sort through your feelings. Many churches have support groups for new mothers, and for seasoned mothers too. Facebook also has hundreds of support groups for mom, although many of them have strict rules for members. Although I despise Facebook, I stay because of a few of the groups I am in. I highly suggest finding one that fits you. There are so many options!

Find out where the mommy guilt stems from. Does it have to do with something from your past or your own childhood? Do you suffer from mommy guilt because you feel bad that there is some way you cannot support your child that you desperately wish you could? Look for other ways you excel as a parent. Focus on what you value as a parent and what type of values you want to instill in your child. Focus on the positive things you are showing your child as opposed to the negative things you might find difficult to control.

CHAPTER TEN

Does My Baby Love Me?

Depending on how you have processed this book so far, you could take this comment one of two ways, but there is a special place deep in my heart for children. I don't necessarily know that I like kids, because if I had the choice to hang out with someone's child or not, or babysit someone's child versus not babysitting someone's child, I would definitely take the latter option. Obviously, I love the children that are in my life, and if I had to go back and do it all again, even after everything I have been through, I would still choose to have kids. I love my kids very much, and also my nieces and nephews, as well as my friends' kids. I don't always like them, but I absolutely love them.

There is such a fine line between loving kids and liking kids, and of course there are parents who won't admit it or don't feel that way, and that's OK, but I know there are a few of you out there reading this book, thinking, *Yes*. Personally, I like things to stay where I put them, I enjoy quiet time, and sometimes I don't want to drop whatever it is I'm doing just because I hear my kid say, "Mom?" Does that mean I ignore my kids? No. Do I cater to my kids? Absolutely. Are they spoiled? Absolutely, and I am secure enough to admit that. Do I go overboard because I feel guilty for everything I went through when Nathan and Nadia were born? One hundred percent. I think because of everything I went through, and knowing that I wasn't emotionally there to support Nathan and Nadia when they were babies, that I overcompensate now. Either that or I just have a really tough time saying no, which certainly could be the case.

When I think of all the kids in the world who might be struggling for one reason or another, the thought breaks my heart. I hate knowing that I can't solve all their problems. I think about the horrific things my husband when through as a child growing up with his parents and the 9-year-old boy who comes into my mother's work and doesn't have enough money on his parents' EBT card to buy a sandwich for breakfast and I am so grateful for everything I have and for everything I can give my kids, even though I went through such an ordeal when they were born.

When I started a new job earlier this year, one of the questions that I was asked during a team building exercise was, "What is one thing you're afraid of?" When it was my turn to answer, I said, "Being poor." The look of horror on the faces of half the people in the room made me question whether or not that is something to actually be afraid of but hear me out. From the moment I had children, I have gone out of my way to work and to be a provider for them. When I was growing up, I wanted for nothing. I had everything I could have needed and mostly everything I wanted. Yes, I am aware that I could have ended up extremely entitled, but I didn't. I was still expected to clean the bathrooms on Saturdays, dust and vacuum the living room, and be home by curfew at midnight. I appreciate everything I was given, and I try to give that back in every way I can to my children and to others as well.

I know that I have gone overboard in spoiling my kids. I know that if I didn't have someone else to be financially responsible to, I would go broke donating school supplies at the beginning of each school year and wrapping up toys at Christmastime. Sometimes I feel so guilty that I am able to provide my kids with what I consider basics, when some parents cannot do the same for their kids. Then I read articles online about parents who, well, frankly, shouldn't be parents and I have to stop myself, because otherwise I will spin down a dark hole that leaves me feeling defeated. When I think of all the kids in foster care, I wish I could do more to support them. If I had the space and a husband who would agree to it, I would be on that in a heartbeat, even if my house was just a safe house they needed to stay in for a while.

Earlier this month, my husband and I were at Nathan's eighth grade completion ceremony with my parents. In front of us was a new mother, her twin baby girls, and what appeared to be grandma. There are so many things about babies that I love, which I know seems so ironic given this book and the fact that I just said I don't always like kids, but it's still true! I'm not sure why, I can't pinpoint a reason, but the outcome doesn't change. I love babies. I love their soft skin, their cute little fingers, and toes, but most importantly, the thing I love about them is the unconditional love they have for their parents.

It makes sense when you really think about it. A baby is literally with their mother 24/7, being carried everywhere. They hear her voice anytime she talks. They get a sense of her, what food she likes, what she doesn't, when she sleeps, her activities, and all the voices of the people she interacts with on a day-to-day basis. That bond is starting to form between the two of them. Sometimes it is immediate and sometimes it isn't; sometimes that process takes time. It isn't always simple, and it isn't always quick, but eventually mother and baby can create that connection. I have experienced both of these two scenarios. Although I prefer the immediate connection, I am grateful to be able to understand both sides of the story.

With Nathan the bond was not immediate, but I was eventually able create it. With Finn, the bond was immediate, and with Nadia, the bond was immediate, but not strong. Simply because I didn't feel that bond with Nathan in the beginning does not mean that it didn't exist or that it wasn't forming over time. Nor did it mean that I should give up on trying to create that tie between us. Even though I didn't feel there was that link initially, it didn't mean he didn't love me or know who I was or vice versa. He still smiled every time he saw my face and he still reached for me to hold him when we were together. He still called me mommy when he first learned the word and I could calm his tears by picking him up and cuddling him when he cried. Although it took me a couple of years to feel that unbreakable bond that was created between the two of us, it doesn't necessarily mean that it didn't exist. I like to think of it more in terms of hibernating. I only regret that I didn't make the extra effort to solidify that bond earlier than the two-year mark.

As for Finn, our attachment was relatively immediate. That pregnancy was so different from mine with Nathan that I often wonder if that was part of the reason we formed that bond so quickly. I was only a few months along when I tore my placenta and had to go on bed rest. The potential to lose him was very real from early on. In addition, I had a conglomeration of other conditions that included placenta previa, carpal tunnel syndrome, high blood pressure, and extreme swelling. Never before had I been so scared. Just the thought that he could be taken away from me so easily was devastating. I cannot imagine the pain of losing a child and God willing, I hope I never have to.

Nadia was somewhere between Nathan and Finn. I had a simple pregnancy with her, other than the extreme nausea. I was throwing up all the time, and my smaller figure while pregnant with her when compared to my other pregnancies was a clear indicator I was definitely not consuming as many calories as I had in the past. I had been working nights during that time, on the same 7/70 schedule I had been working the year prior to her being born. The number of exams I cranked out on that shift is straight up wild, especially since I was the one and only technologist covering a 300-bed hospital all night long until relief came at 6:00 a.m. I was getting my steps in, that's for sure, and not being able to keep my food down unfortunately kept me at a relatively low weight. I was so relieved after she was born because I knew the nauseating feeling I had experienced day in, and day out for the last nine months was soon past.

I can't quite pinpoint the day or week I felt like a bond had been created between the two of us. I know it wasn't immediate, but rather closer to her being three or four months old. Although the bond was beginning to form, it didn't necessarily stop the postpartum depression from taking over. Even with that bond, even though I loved her with my whole heart, even though I would have given my life for her at any moment, I still ended up having postpartum depression. But here's the thing about postpartum depression: it didn't change how she felt about me. Having postpartum depression doesn't mean that your child doesn't love you. Having postpartum depression doesn't mean you aren't worthy of their love. Having postpartum depression doesn't change the fact that you are their mother, their parent, their provider, their everything.

There are so many ways that your baby will show you that they love you. There are many signs that might help ease any worries you have if you are questioning just how much they adore you. Most people, in general, like holding new babies, either because they love babies, they love their new baby smell, they think they are cute, or it reminds them of when their own children were that small and brings back fond memories of that time in their life. For many adults, being able to hold a baby brings them joy, as long as they can give said baby back to their parents as soon as they start screaming or have a dirty diaper. In all seriousness, though, what happens when you hold your own baby? Does she snuggle up to you, as if she is melting into you? Do his eyes light up when you walk into a room? Do they giggle, open their mouth, or smile when you are near? All of these are signs that your baby loves you. Do they stop crying when you pick them up? Your baby wants to keep you close when you are holding them, so they relax in your arms. Your baby is putting their trust in you. When your baby is excited to see you, their physical presence gives you a clue! Their big smile and giggle is a sign of their happiness. That happiness is a sign of their love.

Most babies have a deep-rooted love for their mother the minute they are born, but even those babies that are cared for by someone other than their biological mother can grow attached to the people who regularly show affection to them. If you do not feel like you have that bond with your baby, be a regular presence in their day and provide them with their basic needs of nourishment and love. If I would have stayed home instead of going to work ... if I would have been the one to hold Nathan's bottle ... if I would have been the one who rocked him to sleep ... if I would have made that effort, I would have noticed there was a bond there all along.

What to take away from this chapter:

Babies love their parents. They show their parents this love in many ways. If your baby recognizes you, stares at you, and smiles at you, your baby loves you! If he looks your way when you talk, or mimics noises to get your attention, your baby loves you!

Babies bond with those who provide them nourishment, care, and affection. Your baby will bond to you if you are doing these things. If you do not feel bonded to your baby, even though your baby has clearly bonded with you, see a physician or a nurse practitioner and discuss your feelings. They will be able to help you by giving you advice to try, directing you to a counselor, and/or providing medication that will help balance your hormones and brain chemistry.

CHAPTER ELEVEN

It's Going To Be OK

From time to time, usually when I am in the process of dusting the shelves in my living room, I get caught up in all the photos and find myself sitting on the living room floor looking through family albums from a period of time before the iPhone was widely accepted as a camera. I have this one candid picture that someone took of Nathan and me at his second birthday party. The two of us are in frame as he sits on my lap while opening his presents in the living room. I had just cut my hair into an asymmetrical bob, and I was really slender. The television is on in the background and friends of ours are sitting on the couch behind us. I have a huge smile on my face, and it is clear that I had no idea someone took the picture. It wasn't a staged photo and neither of us were looking at the camera, but both of us were happy.

When everyone asks me how the postpartum ended or when I realized I was better, I always refer back to when Nathan turned two years old. I don't know if this is exactly when things started to get better, or if this is the first time that I remember things were better, but regardless it was around his second birthday when the postpartum started to subside. Dave and I had gotten some pictures taken about a week before his party, because we had finally gotten to a place where we somewhat liked each other again, and I had the same haircut in those pictures as I did with Nathan at his second birthday party. We hadn't taken many pictures together in those two years and I wanted a picture of us to sit on the end table in the living room. This was before selfies were as popular as they are today. I was starting to be more present, my apathetic nature had started to subside, and I wanted a photo to mark that time in our life.

There is this saying by Coco Chanel that is popular on Pinterest: "A woman who cuts her hair is about to change her life." Every time I see that quote, I think of this time period in my life. I don't necessarily think that because I cut my hair my life changed, but rather that the two seemed to coincidentally coincide with each other. When I see this picture of Nathan and I on his second birthday party, my fresh haircut, and the smile on my face, I know that things were on the mend. This isn't to say that I think my hair cut magically made my postpartum depression go away, but rather I am able to put a marker on when I started to feel better, when things started to change, and that was when he was two years old. I wish I could tell you how I got better, or why things got better, but I would be lying if I said I knew. With Nathan, there is no explanation. I didn't go to therapy. I didn't read any books. I didn't even understand what was fully going on with me until I was pregnant with Finn and had time on my hands to really process what I had been through and take the time to understand it all. The truth is, I don't know how or why I got better—I just did, slowly over time.

I have so many fond memories of Nathan and I between 2009 and 2012. It was after the postpartum and before Finn was born. He was really into Thomas the Tank Engine those years. *Hero of the Rails* and *Misty Island Rescue* were staples in our house, and I had so much fun watching him sing to the theme song each time we played one of those movies. The basement was dedicated to his railroad tracks, and every Friday morning when my mom dropped him off back home, he came with a new engine that could. I would sit on the chair in the living room and watch him play with those for tracks for hours. I'm so glad we got that time together.

For a period of time, when my stepdaughter was with her mom, and my stepson was with his, and when Dave was at work, I was with Nathan. We had so many special moments together, just the two of us. We were creating that bond, the one I initially didn't think was there, the one we have still to this day.

If I had to pinpoint what hurt me the most during the time that I had postpartum depression with Nathan and Nadia and the years following was that I didn't talk to someone sooner. I didn't tell my best friend, I didn't tell my parents, I didn't tell a coworker, I didn't tell my doctor and I didn't tell my spouse. I kept quiet and it was the absolute worst thing I did for myself and my family. I would go back and change that decision in a heartbeat if I could. I wasted so much time thinking I was going to be a disappointment to my family. I wasted so much time thinking I couldn't be a good mother because I didn't have this strong bond with my child the minute, I pushed him out. I missed so many moments in Nathan's early years because I didn't think it mattered. I told myself a lie every day for months following Nadia's birth, because I couldn't face the reality that this was happening again. I hadn't been on anti-depressants while pregnant with Nadia since I didn't experience any depression after I gave birth to Finn. There had been such a large time span between Nathan and Nadia, that I honestly didn't think it would happen again. Plus, the lingering question of whether or not the anti-depressants were safe to take while pregnant still held water. When Nadia was born, I didn't want to believe that I was reliving the past, so I ignored the problem completely.

Years later, Dave said something to me. "Imagine watching the person you love most in your life make decisions that you know she will regret later. Image watching that person make decisions, knowing full well that she thinks she is thinking clearly and everyone else in her life is wrong. Image living day in and day out for a year or more, wondering what will today be like. Will she get out of bed today? Will she come home tonight? Will she be manic this week?"

When I think of what I put that man through ... when I think of how much he did for me, for my family, for our family, it brings tears to my eyes. I don't know what kind of mother I would be if I didn't have him by my side. He showed me how to love and care for a newborn. I knew what being a good mother looked like because I watched him be a good father. Of course, this isn't to say that my own parents weren't good examples, because they certainly were, but my memories only go back so far.

I don't know why I got postpartum depression, I don't know if it could have been avoided, and I don't know why it took me years to overcome it. What I do know is that even though I went through years of my life having postpartum depression, there always was help surrounding me. I might not have recognized that help for what it was. I might have subconsciously or consciously pushed that help away, but it was there. I had two parents who stepped in and watched my son overnight four days after he got home from the hospital. I had a sister who would hold Nathan for hours watching television at my house simply so that I could sleep. I had a friend who came over just to sit with me, despite the fact that she was going to be late for work, because I was afraid to be alone with Nathan. I had a primary care physician whom I chose not to say anything to. I had an ob-gyn whom I chose not to say anything to. I had therapists available through the employee assistance program at work, but I didn't reach out. I ignored what I was feeling, and I ignored how I was acting all so I wouldn't have to admit to myself my weakness.

I believe wholeheartedly that timing is everything, and whether you believe that your life is in your own hands, God's hands, or the Universe's hands, things happen when they are meant to. It took me so many years to understand what I had been through. I read so many books, listened to many Ted Talks, and spoke with several doctors before I even began to fully grasp what had happened. But when I think back to the timing of everything that happened in my life, it is so evident that there was a greater plan in store for me. Dave and I got together when I was 23. I graduated from school, got pregnant, had Nathan, and got married. We got married when Nathan was three months old, and we would have never married if we didn't have Nathan. I know Dave didn't want to get married, and honestly, I didn't really like him either, but we had a baby, and we were going to make this family work. I was determined, and thankfully, when I was ready to give up, he wasn't. There was always one of us fighting to stay afloat during every trying time we have been through.

That's the thing about Dave and me. We are a team. What are my strengths are his weaknesses and vice versa. I will fully admit, though, if it weren't for Nathan, we would have ended it. We would have missed a love that we didn't know existed between a husband and a wife. We wouldn't have the family we have today. I may have struggled after giving birth to Nathan, but so many good things came out of it. I am grateful for all the efforts we went through because we have created something between the two of us that can never be dismantled.

As I stated, my story of postpartum depression ended rather anti-climactic with Nathan. Over time, the depression lessened and lessened. Every day, I hoped that the way I was feeling was only temporary. That it was just one day, and I would be better tomorrow. Unfortunately, one day turned into one month, which turned into four and five months, and then into two years. Since I was still able to hold a job, attend family functions, and my child was healthy, I told myself that everything was fine until eventually it was. Please keep in mind that I do not recommend this pathway, but rather I hope you learn from my mistake. Please talk to someone about how you are feeling. Nothing good ever comes out of hiding your mental health struggles.

Over time, I slowly created the bond with Nathan that I was missing in the beginning, the one I wasn't sure was ever going to form. As that bond became evident, it gave me more drive to spend time with him and be the best I could be for him. With Nadia, my postpartum depression started to reach a halt the minute I was able to admit to myself and Dave that something was wrong and I needed help. I might not have felt I had gotten everything I needed from our healthcare system in that moment, but it started my journey of eventually getting the help I needed.

After about a year of taking medication and seeing a therapist, I was able to think clearly for the first time. I thank God I had found a good therapist to talk to, someone I felt was there to give me tools to cope with my feelings and to recognize why I had been feeling and thinking the way I had been feeling and thinking. I know that if I had found a therapist that I didn't feel connected to that I would have given up any hope I had of getting better sooner rather than later. If that does happen to you, and you don't feel like you have a therapist who understands or validates what you are going through, then find a new therapist! If you can't find a therapist in your area that you can get an appointment within a timely manner, start looking online. Betterhelp.com is a great resource with this exact mission in mind.

My hope back then was, and still is, that eventually everything will be OK. I think as I grow older, I still have that same hope. When I was growing up there was a song that was really popular and I would hear it on the radio as I was running errands with my mom, some of my favorite times as a kid. Patty Loveless would play on the radio, singing about how life is always changing and time eases the pain. This song rings true time and time again. As the days turn into weeks and months, my hope is that your pain slowly heals, even though you may never forget what it was that you went through. Even if your story doesn't end the way mine did, or if it isn't your story, there still is something good that can come from each narrative. There is always a lesson that can be learned, enabling you to grow and be a better friend, a better mother, a better spouse, and a better parent.

What to take away from this chapter:

We all know that change doesn't happen overnight. There isn't a magic pill that you can take that will suddenly cure how you have been feeling or change your emotions into something else. Even if there were, I'm sure it would regularly be out of stock. Treatment takes time, and so does healing. Pretending to be OK when you aren't is not the solution. When it comes to mental health, you don't have to "fake it till you make it," and nor should you.

Reflection

After 14 years of being married to my husband, Dave, I have found the life that I envisioned as a little girl. I may have taken the road less traveled to get here, and it may not have been how I planned it was going to go, but I'm finally no longer embarrassed to say that I struggled when I first became a mother. For a long time, I was never able to say this aloud. The worst part was that not only did I struggle, but I struggled in silence, and it was exhausting. I was so scared that the way I was feeling was different than what was "typical" postpartum depression that I felt like I couldn't say anything. I knew depression ran in my family, and I had been on some medications earlier in life, but I didn't think any of that was relevant. I was embarrassed to say how I really felt, and I didn't want to look like I had lost control of my life, shame myself, or humiliate my children.

I am here to tell you that if you are struggling, there is no shame in speaking up, and you don't have to feel isolated or live in silence. You are not alone, and you will not be the last person who ever experiences this, although I wish that were the case. It's OK to say something isn't right, even if you don't know what that something is. There are people who want to help whether you know who those people are or not.

I am not a licensed physician, nurse practitioner, or a mental health professional, although I do have extensive education and experience working in the medical field. I do not claim that sharing what I went through during my own battle with PPD will help you, although I sincerely hope it does. That being said, what I do know is that no matter what you are feeling in this moment, you are not alone and there is someone within reach that wants to help you. Read that again. No matter what you are feeling in this moment, even if you are feeling nothing at all, or don't know what it is you are feeling, you are not alone.

If you do not have any close friends or family to rely on, there are many online support groups, medical professionals, and mental health hotlines that you are able to turn to when you are ready, or even if you aren't. There are people who want to help you. I want to help you, otherwise I wouldn't be sharing these stories. I wish that I knew back then what I know now. I am here to tell you that I got through it and so can you. I will not lie to you and say it will be easy, but I do hope you give yourself a little grace. I hope that I provide you with some clarity and guidance, and help you realize that you can speak up, and that you are stronger than you think you are. I want to remind you that you are good enough, you're doing an excellent job, and no matter what you say, no matter how you feel, your baby loves you, even when you feel you are at your worst.

There is another woman out there at this exact moment who has some of the same feelings that you do. That same woman might even be sitting down somewhere reading a book, or listening to it on audio, searching for that small glimmer of light at the end of a long road, a road she's not even sure will end. Even if you think that what you are experiencing now might be something other than postpartum depression, there is no shame in reaching out to someone about how you are feeling. I wish I had much sooner than I did. If I could go back and do one thing over, it would be that.

References

Ghaedrahmati, M., A. Kazemi, G. Kheirabadi, A. Ebrahimi, and M. Bahrami. 2017. "Postpartum depression risk factors: A narrative review." *Journal of Education and Health Promotion* 6, no. 60. https://doi.org/10.4103/jehp.jehp_9_16.

National Institute of Mental Health. 2022. Perinatal Depression. https://www.nimh.nih.gov/health/publications/perinatal-depression.

Robertson, E., S. Grace, T. Wallington, and D. E. Stewart. 2004. "Antenatal risk factors for postpartum depression: a synthesis of recent literature." *Gen Hosp Psychiatry* 26, no. 4 (Jul-Aug): 289-95. https://doi.org/10.1016/j.genhosppsych.2004.02.006.

www.ingramcontent.com/pod-product-compliance
Lightning Source LLC
LaVergne TN
LVHW052050160826
845678LV00015B/3152